Dream Forest Diary

Childhood in the Penllergare Valley

Anthony James

FOR BRENDA, EMMA, MEG, NICOLE, RACHEL, SORAIYA

Oh as I was young and easy in the mercy of his means,
Time held me green and dying
Though I sang in my chains like the sea.

DYLAN THOMAS

The events described in this book are real and individuals are given their real names when their names are known to me. Fortunately, for most of my life I have enjoyed a very precise and exact memory, and as well as this I have kept detailed diaries and notebooks since early childhood, so that the incidents and conversations in this book are presented with considerable accuracy.

Contents

BEGINNINGS 5

FIRE 11

THE OLD MAN 16

THE VALLEY, THE DECADE
AND THE WORLD 23

SUMMER 29

WINTER 37

LITERATURE AND LAMPLIGHT 43

LAST DAYS 51

THE PARIS TRAIN AND THE BLACK CAT 65

AFTERLIFE 71

ENDING AND BEGINNING 78

BEGINNINGS

At the age of five I saw a more terrifying spectacle than anything I had seen before then in my life. In a huge room, I was confronted by hundreds of strange creatures making a deafening noise and all of them were dangerous and hostile, or so it seemed. It was the autumn of 1961, the beginning of a momentous decade, and for me, the beginning of my life in society. In fact, the room was not huge, it was a classroom of ordinary size in a small village school in South Wales and there were not hundreds of the 'strange creatures', but only thirty or forty, and they were children of my own age who treated me with a mixture of indifference and mild amusement. They were talking and shouting as lively five year-olds do anywhere in the world. We smile, sympathetically or contemptuously, at the impressions of childhood. Yet my perceptions on that wet and misty October morning long ago were real enough to me. Nevertheless, it must have been remarkable, even in 1961, for a child to feel so vulnerable and so terrified on the first day at school. Some other path, not just the stony track through the dripping forest along which I had walked with my mother that morning must have led me to that moment of confusion and terror.

I cried all that day, and the next and the next. Into my grey world of misery came Miss Thomas, the class teacher. She was tall, had long dark hair and she was attractive – but I thought of her as beautiful, because she seemed to me to be a kind of goddess of superhuman goodness, and the long red dress she was wearing the first time I saw her tended to strengthen this impression.

I grew up in the Valley Woods of Penllergare, about five miles northwest of Swansea in South Wales, once a gentry estate. My only sibling, my brother, was nine years older than me. In my childhood, the Valley Woods was an extremely remote place and the only other house, Middle Lodge, was about a quarter of a mile away, people lived there a short time and left. Three girls of about my age did live in Middle Lodge in summer 1961, but my shyness and the fact that they were girls meant that I hardly saw them for over a year. They left in 1963, and no other children lived in the valley.

My mother and father tended to be reclusive and we had very little extended family, so I had no cousins near to my own age. I was sensitive and introverted and I only saw other children at a distance when I went shopping in Swansea with my mother. These are the bare facts – the path along which I travelled to my morning of terror in the village school. There is also the fact that I loved – and still love – the valley of my childhood. Miss Thomas, the class teacher, was important enough in my childhood to give me a lasting respect for women and for female values and an appreciation of the general strength and decency of women. The valley woods was an even more profound and many-sided influence, but the word influence is very abstract and the real task is to make the past real in the present...

I am sitting on the grass in the sunlight, a pale, fresh sky above me. Everything is bright and delicate, the colour of the grass and the colour of the sky, and behind me is deep shadow near the brown sandstone wall of the house. My mother has just carried me out of the house and has turned back to do something near the door. It must be spring or very early summer, because there are not many insects in the air, not much is moving across my line of vision as I stare across the valley in front of me into the distance and see dark patches of pine forest. There is a soft blanket of quietness traced with birdsong lying over everything, something that is difficult to find in Britain today. Beyond the grass is the track that runs from one end of the valley to the other, called 'the drive' by my parents. For me, that morning is the beginning of the world, the beginning of consciousness and I have no earlier memories than this one. I think I must have been about two and a half years old on that day, and I have the impression that later that day and on the following days, more and more words that I knew were floating around me like invisible but solid objects in the air. On one of the following days, the weather has turned rough and stormy and the sky is grey and also tawny orange because the sun's rays are colouring the clouds. My mother and I are eating cold meat and potato pie for lunch, there is a bottle of Worcestershire sauce on the table and the orange label on the bottle strikes me as almost the same colour as the clouds.

There was nothing unchanging or 'timeless' about the valley in which I grew up. The morning I sat on the grass in the sunlight in my earliest memory was probably the spring of 1959 and the Penllergare

Valley Woods was changing and evolving, a process that continues to this day. The valley had once been a nineteenth century designed landscape, by 1959 the Dillwyn Llewelyn family was long gone and the valley was fast reverting to the natural wilderness it had been at some more remote time. In January 1961 the 'Big House' of the estate, already decaying and vandalised, was blown up. On a Saturday afternoon I followed my mother around the bend in 'the drive' at which the house became visible and found army vehicles and uniformed soldiers already there. I looked in awe because Saturday afternoon was the time to visit the toyshops in Swansea, I already loved model vehicles, especially model army vehicles and now I was face to face with the real thing. On the following day the house was blown up, demolished, in the late morning, I think. To my great regret at the time, I did not see this happening. It seemed that we could hear a distant boom and roar from our house, but I may be mistaken about this.

We lived in Upper Lodge and the nearest inhabited house to ours was Middle Lodge, the houses had passed to a family in the village and we rented our home from them. I have never known with certainty the reasons for the decision that my parents made to live in Upper Lodge. My father was born in 1900 and my mother in 1919, families communicated less in those days and the motives of parents were not often questioned or explained. The scenes, always vivid, become more numerous and frequent...

Perhaps it was the same summer of 1959. The stillness and glare of the heat lay softly and heavily on the valley and we walked on the path between the expanses of rhododendrons with the noise of insects throbbing on our ears. At last, we came to the edge of a sloping field with a tall, wind-twisted pine standing out from the forest along the edge of the field. And rearing up in the heat shimmer at the top of the sloping field was a house, quite a beautiful house, white with bright yellow window frames and doors, the bright colours of a fairy story or a folk tale, and empty, uninhabited. Away on the right, matted with ivy, was the crumbling stonework of the Walled Gardens, slipping away, month by month into the undergrowth and the bristling young trees. The garden of the house itself, though overgrown now, was bright with orange and yellow flowers, which we picked, in the strange, vibrating hush that lay over everything. I was told that a

Swedish couple had lived for a time in the house, and my parents mundanely called it 'Swede's House' and the field 'Swede's Field', perhaps with a touch of unexplained hostility. Some kind of sadness or misfortune attached itself to the place. Strangely, this beautiful house was not lived in through the years of my childhood and its decay kept pace, year by year, with my own growth. The white walls flaked and turned a dull brown, the bright window frames rotted away, the roof fell in and the garden was choked. Like the Anglo-Saxon settlers of the sixth century A.D., living near to decaying Roman towns and villas, relentlessly being reclaimed by wild growth, I grew up among the crumbling remains of the past. Today, the ruin of 'Swede's House' lies somewhere a few steps beyond the kitchens, bathrooms and streets of a modern housing estate, although a large expanse of the valley and its forests remain.

One evening in that summer we were sitting outside the house on that same expanse of grass on which I had been set down by my mother in my earliest memory. The drive was still passable for ordinary vehicles in those days and a car drove past us, on down towards Middle Lodge. I think it was owned by whoever lived in that house at that time, as I have said, people came and went, whereas we remained in Upper Lodge year after year. The car was wide and light blue with a white roof and I was struck by the way in which the colours matched those of the sky on this clear evening, with the sun getting low and a small bank of high, delicate clouds near the horizon. I also recall some faintly disapproving remark about the owner of the car. I did not know it then, but my parents had lived through the terrible bombing of Swansea during the Second World War, among the worst in Britain, probably the most momentous experience of their lives. Britain in the 1950s was a place of rapid change and flux and the changes reached even as far as the Penllergare Valley. People born in far distant countries were to be seen in Britain as never before, after all, the war had disrupted an entire continent and an entire world. Were there tensions that affected the attitudes of my parents? About this time I asked my father, rather comically, about the world. We had walked far down the valley towards the tiny village of Cadle Mill, past the lake. There is a point at which you can look back in the direction of our house, northwards, with the west side of the valley rising to your left and forming a continuous curve with forest to the north beyond the lake and the low rolling hills to the east and south.

'So that's it!' I shouted excitedly. 'That's the world! Is that the world?' I had heard, some time not long before that day, that the world is round.

'No, no. That's just as far as you can see.'

'But can we get to somewhere where we can see the whole world?' I had the vague sense of having been on the edge of a wonderful discovery, which was slipping out of my grasp.

'No, it's too big, you can't see it all at once.'

Ten years later, human beings walked on the moon and looked at the earth from its surface and mine was the first generation to see the earth in that way.

The summer passed and I remember little about the following winter. I do remember one evening towards the end of that winter, it must have been late February. I had been ill – I was often ill as a child – and I had been eating little. Now I was given two large boiled potatoes with some bread and butter, they had been cooked for my father's evening meal the night before but not served because he had not wanted more. The fact that the potatoes had come from the previous evening and had been warmed up for me made them particularly appealing for some reason. As I ate I looked out of the window beside the table at the grey clouds being torn and driven by a strong wind as night began to fall and a large number of rooks flew over the house, wheeling and changing direction in the wind, making a collective rattling cry that could be heard inside the house. At that moment I was filled with an extraordinary happiness and contentment that I can feel even now as I write.

Nine years later, as a boy of twelve, I stood at the bottom of Swede's Field with the spring storms and sunlight chasing each other in circles down the valley, feeling an enormous sadness and apprehension. I had been sent out to exercise the dogs while frantic activity went on back at the house, and I knew that everything had changed and our life here in the valley was over, so that it was one of those moments when the present already seems like the past. Throughout my childhood in that strange valley I had been surrounded by the reminders of enormous changes and now huge changes had come to my own life and I realised then, for the first time, that some of the sadness in life is due to the fact that things are always changing. The moments of happiness are driven off like the clouds or fly way like the rooks. If we are fortunate, memory is vivid, clear and exact, and if we are very, very fortunate, we may be able to make the past real for others.

FIRE

Danger and frightening situations creep up on us, and how normal and innocent everything seems just before they do. It was a mild Sunday morning in the September before my eighth birthday, with the sun gleaming like a butter-coloured patch on the overcast sky and the grass wet with dew. My mother and father and I were up early and my mother was grumbling about how difficult the fire in the grate was to get started and my father was grumbling into his tea and over his pipe that the bacon and eggs for breakfast were a long time in coming.

I was quite hungry too, but the fresh air was far more appealing than the steamy kitchen full of the complaining of adults and I went out into the glistening morning and forgot about food as I fought and killed imaginary enemies with a wooden sword. Such childhood battles are timeless, but it must have been about ten minutes before I suddenly turned and looked back at the house anxiously, not knowing why I did so. Something was wrong, very wrong. Slim and narrow jets of black smoke were rising from the brick chimney above the slate roof and mixed with them were devilish looking spikes of dark orange flame, other equally cruel looking tongues of flame were forcing their way out through the gaps between the brickwork of the chimney. I ran back into the house and there was a dread in my stomach that came from the conviction that this was somehow more serious than I could properly understand.

'There's fire coming out of the chimney!'

My father was not a man who was easily moved to panic, especially not early in the morning with a cup of tea in front of him, and I think that, in any case, he thought that my shouts about fire were part of the game I was playing. My mother, however, hurried back outside with me and across the expanse of grass, now wet, on which she had set me down in my earliest memory. When she saw the chimney, she screamed in a way I had never heard before and then called out for my father with the same note in her voice, so that flame tips of fear, seeming as real as the flames coming from the chimney, touched the insides of my stomach.

My father came blinking into the open air, a bald-headed, broad, strong man with his braces hanging down alongside his legs. I saw his face change as he looked at the chimney and I saw that the flames had forced their way further out of the brickwork and were licking at the beam that ran from the base of the chimney between the slates, dividing the roof into two parts on that side of the house.

'Bring buckets of water!' he roared at my mother. I had seen my father angry, but I had never seen him frightened, or even particularly alarmed at anything, he was not a nervous or a sensitive man. I began to cry now, because his fear terrified me. However slow he had been to react before, he moved swiftly enough now, a man approaching sixty-four, in bad health, with a persistent cough.

He ran to the lean-to shed beside the house and picked up the wooden ladder that was kept there and swung it up crashing against the edge of the roof. With the quickness of a fox or a cat he was up on the slates, bellowing for water. There was also something terrifying in the speed at which he moved, I had always known him as a deliberate, stubborn, pipe smoking man, with a bad chest. I began to cry more freely from fear as our German shepherd Prince came out of the house, stretching unconcernedly, looking with indifference at the scene, and then shifting on his paws uneasily as the mood of the human beings communicated itself to him. My mother came out then, carrying two buckets of water. My brother had not yet appeared. He worked during the week and was no doubt intent on a lie in, and if the shouting had woken him, he may well have thought that I had provoked my parents by breaking or upsetting something.

'Go to Mrs Jones at the Home Farm!' my father yelled at me as my mother was climbing the ladder behind him with one of the buckets. 'Tell her what's happened! Tell her to let you phone the Fire Brigade!'

We had no vehicle of our own. Mobile phones did not exist, and in 1964 far from every house, even those of prosperous families, had a telephone. There was no telephone at Middle Lodge.

'I don't know how to use the telephone!' I wailed desolately and quite truthfully.

'Mrs Jones will phone them.' my mother told me, coming down for the other bucket. 'Go on!'

And so I went running off, up the stone steps, through our neglected back garden that merged imperceptibly with the woodland, along the paths that wound through the rhododendrons. The sun was starting to come out and the moisture on the grass shone, but for me everything seemed poisoned with dread and menace, the familiar sights looked hideous. Swede's Field, Swede's House, the old kennels, thick with ivy and disappearing into the undergrowth, the lane leading up to Home Farm. I also suffered with a bad chest and I was a poor runner and I could only run in short bursts, and as well as this, anxiety must have tightened my chest and made breathing difficult. I would have much preferred to have been allowed to stay and fight the fire, rather than being sent on this mission, not knowing whether my home was burning down behind me. My empty stomach churned with fear and with the jolting of my bursts of running. Then at last, the Home Farm was in sight.

I knocked on the door, used the knocker, pounded on the cracked paint of the door with my fist, paused to listen, and began knocking again. Panic was rising in me and I began to cry again. I had the sensation of thumping on the house as you would thump on a large, empty wooden box. Dimly, through the panic, I began to remember some remark I had heard from someone about a week ago, something about Mrs Jones going on holiday or to stay with relatives, I also had some recollection of being told that she went every year. It was not the kind of information that would have interested me. Until now! I barely noticed Mrs Jones except for when she talked to my mother and occasionally told me something interesting about animals or gave me sixpence. The farm was no longer a working farm and she lived alone in the farmhouse. I peered in through the window and knocked once again, but without hope.

I went a few steps back the way I had come and then turned and started off towards the village and once again stopped. Should I go back and tell my parents that I had failed? Should I go on to the village and raise the alarm there? They had not told me to go any further, did that mean that it was better to go back and help to carry buckets, rather than stay away any longer? I desperately wanted to know if my home was still standing and if my family was safe. I was not quite eight years old and the decision was proving to be beyond me. As I stood agonizing and undecided, I heard a sound.

Around the bend in the lane that led to the village came a man on a motor scooter. By that time in my life I had already developed the skill of slipping out of sight almost as quickly as a wild animal, but I stood still and let the man ride past me. I was not sure whether he saw that something was wrong by the way I looked, as he was riding quite slowly, or just wanted to ask directions. Whatever the reason, he turned in a wide arc and rode back to me.

I had been warned not to talk to strangers, but perhaps this was an exception. He wore the helmet with leather earflaps and the goggles that were usually worn by riders of motorcycles and motor scooters in those days.

'I say, is the place where the old mansion used to be near here?' He sounded very English, very educated. I began to cry again.

'Something wrong?' the man asked.

'My house is on fire and they sent me to get Mrs Jones to phone the Fire Brigade, but she's not here.'

'Oh well, look here, I'll ride back into the village and phone the Fire Brigade from there and you get along back. They've probably got it under control by now.'

Relief washed up from my feet and into my chest as I heard this. Also, the man sounded so invincibly cheerful that I felt he could somehow make his words come true just by saying them.

'Thank you! Thank you!'

'What's the name of your house? What's the address?'

'Upper Lodge.'

'Right! Got that! You'd best be getting back.'

He rode off, and I began to run on aching and stiffening legs back the way I had come. I knew exactly the place at which I would be able to see the house, and as I reached it, I gathered myself, as if to receive a savage physical blow. Then I stood still and stared. The house was intact and unharmed, or at least, the broad roof of slates was still on and there was no sign of smoke or flames.

I ran down the steps and around the house. Two young men with cartridge belts around their waists and shotguns propped up against the fence had formed a human chain with my father on the ladder, and my mother brought them buckets of water. From this side of the house, I could see that the base of the chimney was still smoking and sputtering and part of the beam had been blackened by fire. Inside the house, Prince, our German shepherd barked furiously because of the presence of strangers.

It seemed that minutes after I had left, my brother had been sent off to North Lodge, where Mrs Nozicka lived, to call for the Fire Brigade from there. The two young men who were shooting in the valley had appeared soon after this and had immediately stopped to help. Sending my brother and myself in different directions had been a sensible move on the part of my parents – those who could run were sent to get help and those who could not run stayed and tried to put the fire out.

I heard the concentrated roar of a large vehicle further up the drive and the fire engine arrived. I watched in awe and admiration as the firemen jumped out of the still moving vehicle and extended the ladder and hose with amazing speed. The next minutes passed in enjoyable wonder as water was pumped down the chimney from outside and up the chimney from inside the kitchen. I was a child, and now that the fear had drained away, I found the whole thing exciting, having no conception of mess, disruption, work and fatigue. I had forgotten my own weariness and my own terror.

After some serious conversation about what must be done to make the chimney safe before the fire could be lit again, the firemen left. The driver of the fire engine, a man with a heavy, grey moustache, sweated and stripped down to his white cotton singlet as he backed and turned the huge vehicle, churning up a part of the grassy expanse by the house as he did so.

I never knew whether the phone call from the man on the motor scooter was made before my brother had raised the alarm at North Lodge or afterwards.

'I know what I want for my birthday.' I told my mother that afternoon.
'Yes, I can guess. You want a model fire engine.'
As a matter of fact, I wanted a real fire engine, an axe, a helmet and a uniform, but I would settle for the model if it was large enough.

THE OLD MAN

It was the half term holiday in February in the following year. The morning was sharp-edged with frost, but the sky was a glowing blue and the sunshine clear and abundant, and spring seemed to have come to the valley early on that day. I was up and about and my father was still in bed and I heard sounds coming from the bedroom next to mine. The evening before I had made a cardboard mask that had accidentally turned out far more terrifying than I had intended. I went to the doorway of the bedroom in which my parents slept, taking the mask with me, finding my father still asleep and talking aloud in the middle of some dream. Then I put the mask on and called to him. He slowly opened his eyes and then stared at me in horror, and for only the second time in my life I saw my father frightened. I took the mask off and laughed uneasily.

'Boy...It's you.' he said wonderingly. 'I thought – I thought it was an old man.'

The vision must have been all the more terrifying because I was no taller than the average eight year-old.

Three quarters of an hour later, breakfast eaten, we were outside in the sunshine and the wooden handcart my father had made was leaning on its shafts against the sandstone wall of the house. He was applying grease to the axles of the metal wheels and my job was to keep the wheel turning as he did so. I was a child who was prone to daydreaming and my thoughts often drifted off and they did so now. The wheel turned more and more slowly and stopped.

'Keep turning him, boy.' my father said tersely. At least he didn't tell me to 'wake up' as my teachers often did. Miss Thomas of the reception class had long ago been left behind and teachers grew stricter and less patient as I grew older.

We set off, with my father pulling rather than pushing the handcart by its shafts, the metal wheels grinding harshly on the overgrown stones and gravel of the drive. Under the overhanging trees the air had a cold tang. On the cart were my father's saw and a five-gallon can. As we had no vehicle, the cart, which my father had built himself, was a fairly sensible accessory. None of us wanted to simply carry the supplies we needed a mile and a half or so from the village, or carry the loads of firewood that we needed continually from parts of the valley nearer to our house. My father's chest was in a bad condition, and partly because of the cold air he stopped to cough and to rest fairly frequently.

'Why do we live in the woods?' I asked during one of our halts.

'Don't you like living in the woods?' Trust an adult to answer a question with a question.

'Yes.' I said slowly. My father waved a hand in a ravelled woollen glove at the sunlit valley and forest.

'All this was once the country estate of the Dillwyn Llewelyn family.'

'So what happened to them?'

'One of them died in a shooting accident – the son.'

'And the father?'

'He died too, in 1927, I believe.'

'Why?'

'Why? Well, he was an old man, boy.'

We went on and finally came in sight of the big house of the Dillwyn Llewelyn family, or rather what was left of it, as it had been blown up by the army in January 1961. The rubble and broken timber extended over an area the size of a small field, with pits and hollows, and now, over four years after the demolition, it was much grown over by vegetation. Trees hemmed in the shattered remains of the house on three sides and the drive wound past it on the fourth side. On the other side of the drive was a clearing and beyond that was more woodland with a huge, sharp-spiked monkey puzzle tree rearing upwards above everything else.

My father had seen a particularly thick and heavy piece of timber in the rubble some days before, just the kind of wood that burns slowly and gives a great deal of heat, ideal fuel for us, and now he began to saw it free. I wandered off, climbing over the rubble and exploring. Soon I heard voices and crept forward. Two girls and two boys from the village who were the same age as myself were ahead of me, playing and exploring. I knew them all quite well and I was tempted to go and join them, but I hung back. A beam of monstrous size stuck out of the rubble at an angle, its end about eight feet from the ground. One of the boys had got about halfway up the beam and a girl called Julie was trying to follow him up.

'I can't get up!' Julie wailed and the boy reached down and dragged her up to the place he had reached. I felt a sort of indignant contempt at Julie's poor performance at climbing, having climbed to the top of the beam more than once myself. Girls were truly silly! Half a minute later, however, the second girl who was called Anne climbed up and dragged both Julie and the boy down and then triumphantly climbed to the very top of the beam herself. Unlike Julie, who had a skirt on, Anne was wearing jeans. Girls, I decided, were frightening when they were not silly because they could do as much as boys could do – or more. Secretly and grudgingly, I liked most of the girls better than the boys, but according to the social norms of the village school in those days I could not make friends with them. It was acceptable for equal numbers of boys and girls to go out in a small gang like this one on special occasions, or for a particularly brave and tough girl to tag along with a gang of boys. But for a boy to have girls as his friends was 'sissy'.

I made my way back to where my father was still methodically sawing and began to throw bits of dried moss at him, so that they bounced off his back.

'Hey! Stop that!'

I kept at a safe distance and hurled more moss at him and he peered at me over his shoulder, little red patches of anger forming around his eyes. When I guessed that he had calmed down enough, I approached him and asked him to let me try sawing. He agreed with a grunt. I found the work amazingly hard and attacked the wood in a near frenzy.

'Too wild, boy, too wild. Push and let the saw go of itself. Put the force into the forward stroke and just draw it back lightly.'

And of course it worked! In my childhood, my father taught me to use a saw, just as he sometimes let me fire his gun, a beautiful bolt-action cartridge gun. I grew up to be someone comfortable with saws, timber, sharp tools, firearms, and large, powerful dogs, and this was to prove important more than once in later life.

When the wood was finally sawn free, we loaded it onto the cart and then my father sat down and began to smoke his pipe. I sat on a large oblong block of masonry near him, my legs swinging.

'I'm never going to get married!' I said, thinking of Julie and Anne.
'You will, boy, you will.'
'I won't if I don't want to!' I said fiercely, but my father chuckled into his pipe, his face had taken on that remote and benign expression which the faces of pipe smokers tend to assume as they become engrossed in a pipe.
'That's the trouble, boy, you'll want to. You'll want to!'
After he had finished smoking, we went on up the drive, turning left at the place where the circular stone building which had been the astronomical observatory crouched, alien and mysterious among dark, overhanging trees.
'Why didn't we get the wood on the way back?' I asked when he next stopped to rest and cough, leaning forward and resting his arms against the cart, the sunlight making the leather strip across the shoulders of his old jacket gleam.
'Might not feel like it then.'
'Are we going to the Old Inn?' I asked with great interest. 'Are you going to drink beer?'
'That's right.'
'Well, what difference does it make? Why not go to the Old Inn first and cut the wood on the way back?'
'Well, boy, the man who has to drink before he does his work is probably not going to get through the day.'

The drive passed between open fields now, and patches of scrubby meadow, then we were approaching North Lodge. There was a long, low building joined onto the house and my father abruptly turned the cart off the drive and out of the sunlight and into the shadows behind this building, which had once been a schoolroom. I heard the barking of dogs coming nearer and nearer and around the corner of the building came Mr Nozicka, tapping a length of copper pipe pointedly against his thigh. Mr Nozicka, who lived in North Lodge, was a Czech, a tall, lean man with a proud, sad, deeply lined face.
'Hey, what you think you do?' he shouted at my father. 'I put up PRIVATE sign!'
My father turned to face Mr Nozicka, eyeing him coldly, and at Mr Nozicka's side a German shepherd and a black Labrador barked with such fury that saliva flew from their mouths.
'I don't give a damn about you or your PRIVATE sign.' my father

said slowly and precisely. The two men looked at each other through a long, still moment.

'Good wood you got there, Jack.' Mr Nozicka said suddenly, peering down at the cart. 'Where you get that?'

'Ah, you have to know where to look.' my father told him. Mr Nozicka turned abruptly on the infuriated dogs.

'Shut up your mouths!' The dogs instantly fell silent and my father lifted the five-gallon can down off the cart. My mother and Mrs Nozicka were friends, but my father's relationship with Mr Nozicka was more complicated.

'We're going into the village. Pick this lot up on our way back.' My father nodded at the cart.

'No school today, Tony? You help the old man, yes?' Mr Nozicka asked me, pronouncing my name 'tawny'.

'I cut some of that wood. And he's not an old man, he's my father.' I said with studied insolence. Mr Nozicka tipped his head back and laughed loudly, the sound bouncing back off the stones of the walls in the shadows.

'Another one like you, Jack, I think!'

The drive ended here at North Lodge and we turned out onto the main road that led towards Morriston and walked towards the crossroads and the roundabout at the centre of the village. The garage stood here, not much like a service station today, a couple of petrol pumps and two large sheds to one side of a big, square house that was later demolished. Mr Wynford John and his father Jack John, who always dressed in a long brown overall coat, moved about and nodded in greeting to my father. In the furthest of the sheds was the paraffin tap, connected to a large container outside the wall of the shed, the supply of the fuel that gave us light and to some extent heat. Knowing my father so well, they let him fill the five-gallon can himself. I shall always remember that shed! The light was not good, and one end usually stood open to the air, so that in winter it was bitterly cold, with tools, spare parts, broken parts, strange and bulky batteries in brightly coloured casing, objects that had uses I could hardly guess at, all covered with an ancient, well used oiliness and griminess. Such were garages in those days! My father paid for the paraffin and then took the big can to the back of the shed, like our cartload of timber, it was to be left and returned for later.

Now we crossed the road to the Old Inn and I felt immensely proud, grown up and independent to be walking into a pub with my father, even the words 'pub' and 'beer' carried a faint suggestion of wickedness, danger, mystery and the carefree world of grown men where you could do as you pleased. The bar was long and smoky, dim after the bright February sunlight, with a handful of men sitting or standing, two of them greeting my father.

'Got some help today, Jack.'

'Aye.'

'Never known Jack James to need help to drink his beer.'

'Never known you to drink beer without needing help to walk.'

There was a faint ripple of slightly uneasy chuckling, after this, my father did not choose to notice the existence of the man who had made the joke, having answered him without turning to look at him, and I was pleased to adopt the same scornful manner. This was the life! The middle-aged lady behind the bar glanced at me and raised her eyebrows, but said nothing. My father bought a pint of bitter for himself and a glass of lemonade for me. I stood at the bar beside my father without talking, savouring the moment, a moment in which the Old Inn was no longer just the village pub, it was just as much a saloon in a dangerous township in the Old West and I was a seasoned adventurer who had walked in after crossing hundreds of miles of wilderness. Mr Ron Williams the landlord came through from the private part of the pub and into the bar and nodded to my father, then turned to me.

'Good afternoon to you, sir.'

'Good afternoon.' I said solemnly. Yes, the saloonkeeper was a good man, he knew my reputation as a gunfighter and treated me with proper respect.

My father bought a second pint of bitter for himself and another lemonade for me and we took the drinks out into the little porch of the pub where there were wooden benches fixed to the walls. Either my father had become bored in the bar or, more likely, despite being a smoker himself, the stuffy atmosphere had affected his chest. Now that we were in the open air, he lit his pipe.

'Can I try some beer?'

'No!'

'Just a little taste?'

'You're too young.'
'Just a little bit. I've never tasted it.'
'There's men who have been drinking it for forty years who have never tasted it.'
Nevertheless, he poured a tiny amount of beer from his glass into my lemonade. I didn't really like the beer or its strange, raw smell because it made the lemonade taste sour, but I pretended to enjoy it. This was a memorable day!
'Don't tell your mother!'
When our second drinks were finished, my father returned the glasses to the bar and we crossed the road and collected our can of paraffin from the garage, my father leaning sideways as he carried it because of the weight. At North Lodge he loaded the can onto the cart and we set off for home.

The sky was changing amazingly quickly, the sunlight and the bright blue were being replaced by a dull, chilling grey, as if the air above us was being coloured over by a giant pencil. A freezing damp rolled up the valley from the south, from the direction of Swansea and the coast. My father coughed with a racking sound. A long way beyond the rubble of the big house, we stopped to rest at a place where the secretive roar of the waterfall in the gorge below us rose up and mixed with the rustling of the trees.
'You didn't fight in the war, did you?' I asked for some reason.
'No, too old to be called up for the regular army, I was in the Home Guard a bit.'
'You didn't fight the Germans though.'
'Would have fought them, I suppose, if they'd invaded this country.' My father took the opportunity to take out his pipe and fill it, the yellow box of matches seeming an unusually bright, glowing colour in the grey light that had spread across the valley.
'Lots of people were killed in the war, weren't they?'
'Yes, many people. There were American soldiers stationed in the big house back there.'
'Perhaps there'll be another war and I'll be killed.'
My father struck a match, the flame wavered and steadied and his pipe glowed, a tiny pocket of fire in the slate grey landscape.
'No, I don't think so, boy, I think you'll live to be an old man.'

THE VALLEY, THE DECADE
AND THE WORLD

At the Dan-yr-Ogof Showcaves in the Upper Swansea Valley there is a Shire Horse Centre that includes the reconstruction, room by room, of the Welsh hill farm that was the home of the Morgan brothers in the early 1900s. In the kitchen stands an Aladdin paraffin lamp, identical to the one that lighted the kitchen and living room of my childhood home in the 1960s, so that when I first took my daughter Emma to the Shire Horse Centre as a very little girl, I was able to show her something that made my early years real to her. Upper Lodge, the house I lived in until I was twelve, had no electricity and therefore no television. I could not share in the television culture of the other children at primary school, something that increased my sense of separation from them.

However, we did have a radio and it was considered almost indecent in our house to fail to listen to the radio news at least twice a day. A child growing up in such a place before the invention of radio would have been enormously more cut off from the world. It seems strange, almost surreal, to me now to think of that house with its primitive conditions standing in the vast silence of the forest and fields, often cut off by bad weather, but receiving this stream of information about the incredible changes and upheavals of the wider world.

Something else in my childhood that was as significant as the lack of electricity was the age of my parents. My mother was between ten and fifteen years older than the parents of most of the children who went to school with me, and my father was between thirty and thirty-five years older than those parents. Therefore, the generation gap – I believe this term was first used in the 1960s – was much larger, with the result that my parents were less sympathetic to much of what was new in that extraordinary decade than most parents. I was a bright child, and having a brother who was nine years older than myself meant that I lived for most of my childhood in the valley with three adults and listened to their conversations and arguments. From the radio came some idea of the dread, fear and pessimism that gripped many people in those years when they thought about the possibility of nuclear war. My parents were unsympathetic to these concerns, partly because they had lived through a war in which this country had been threatened by a terrible enemy in the east and had survived by standing firm. They also lived through the war in one of the most severely bombed areas in Britain. I don't say that their attitude was right or realistic, but it was real enough to them.

My parents were old enough and aware enough to have seen clearly the deadly danger that faced Britain in 1940 and to have responded to the sense of purpose and hope that Churchill brought to the situation, this was particularly true of my mother. She had a book of Churchill's speeches and would sometimes read to me from it, and as well as this, parts of the speeches were still quite often broadcast on the radio in those days. Even today, I can still recite at least two of Churchill's wartime speeches from memory. Reminders of the war were around us in the valley, American soldiers had been stationed in and near the Dillwyn Llewelyn big house. Mr Nozicka, who lived in North Lodge, was a Czech and was probably acquainted with some of the worst events of modern European history.

Another event that made an enormous impression on my mother was the war that Finland had to fight when attacked by the Soviet Union in 1939, as well as the courage of the Finns, much praised by Churchill, outnumbered by fifty to one. This event would have meant much less to her if she had not already had a passion for classical music, including the music of the Finnish composer Sibelius. As we had no electricity, we could not have a record player, but there was BBC Radio 3, called the Third Programme in those days, through which my own love of classical music developed. It was because of Sibelius and my mother's memories of 1939 that I became increasingly interested in Finland and taught myself to read Finnish in early adult life. One of my major interests as a writer has been translating and writing about Finnish literature. As an adult, I travelled extensively in Finland, the most densely forested country in Europe, a very suitable place for someone who grew up in the Penllergare Valley Woods! My own passion for modern history and my love of travel began with the enormous significance of the war in my mother's life. She talked compulsively about anything that interested her – a characteristic that has been passed on to me, as my wife knows only too well. I have spent much of the last twenty-five years in travelling to the places I heard about in childhood, across Europe from Ireland to the Czech Republic, from Arctic Norway to southern Greece and to North Africa and Russia. Also, living in the valley seemed almost like living in a separate country to me in my childhood.

Ironically, perhaps, I never learned Welsh, although my father spoke Welsh fluently. I recall my father saying with some pride, more than once during my childhood, that he was capable of writing an entire letter in grammatically correct Welsh, but he made little or no effort to teach me the language. My mother is English and knew no Welsh, and only English was spoken in our home.

My mother regarded herself as a convinced Christian, while my father was noncommittal. However, my mother was decidedly a bible Christian and we rarely attended St David's Church in the village. Despite, or perhaps because of this, I always knew bible stories and verses from the bible better than any of the other children, at least at primary school, sometimes quoting them well enough to astonish my teachers. On Sunday mornings and Sunday evenings, as we got nearer to Home Farm, crossing Swede's Field, we could hear the sound of the church bells in the village, blending in summer with the birdsong. As an adult, I have not been a religious person, but any religious feelings I have experienced were bound up with the natural world.

The radio was such an integral part of my life that it seems strange that I hardly ever listen to it now. Between the 1960s and the 1980s it used to be said that everyone remembered where they were when they heard that President Kennedy had been assassinated. Although I was so young, I remember that too. We were sitting at the kitchen table and had just finished eating on that November day in 1963 when the announcement came. Rather callously perhaps, my parents seemed most preoccupied with the fact that the flawless professionalism of the radio announcer, which they had no doubt become so used to during the war, slipped under the shock of the news and he gasped, voice shaking and there was a prolonged silence in the studio.

Some programmes were part of our daily lives, for instance the series called *The Archers,* which was not a very impressive drama in those days and so gave me a lifelong dislike and awareness of stilted dialogue, stodgy characterisation and predictable plots. Still, the series was set in and around a small country village and one of the storylines concerned the Development Plan, a massive proposed project of building and modernisation that would affect the lives of all the characters. The first phase of building in the Penllergare valley in my lifetime began in the middle of the 1960s, and fields and meadows on the edge of the village became a housing estate, so that this was one aspect of the story that I could relate to well. I grew up with an awareness that remote places are fragile and vulnerable. Also, the valley was placed between two large urban areas and not all of those who came there were pleasant characters, so that my own attitudes to conservation have been shaped by the experience of seeing needlessly killed or injured animals and vandalism in the woods.

A great many comedy programmes found their way onto the radio in the 1960s and so found their way into our home. *Hancock's Half Hour, The Goons, Steptoe and Son, Beyond our Ken, The Navy Lark, The Clitheroe Kid* and Ken Dodd, the array of British humour that came before the revolution marked by *Monty Python's Flying Circus.* Some of it was funny, but some of it seemed monumentally unfunny to me, partly because it was modern and *urban* humour with which I could make very little mental connection, though the children who went to school with me, who saw some of these shows on television, could probably relate them much more easily to their own lives.

In 1966, through his own efforts and determination, my brother John got a ticket for the World Cup Final at Wembley where England played West Germany and I listened to the live commentary on the radio with my parents. July 30 1966 was an overcast afternoon in the valley and I can recall my father, a soccer enthusiast rather than a rugby enthusiast, visibly sweating with excitement as he listened to the radio – since Wales could not win the World Cup, the next best thing was a victory for England. Once again, I had a surreal sense of dislocation and remoteness as I reflected that somewhere in the roar of thousands of people behind the commentator's voice was my brother who had started out from this house extremely early that morning. I think that sense of strangeness would not have existed if

I had lived in an ordinary home and watched the match on television.

The aspect of sixties culture that entered our home through the radio and made the greatest impact of all, and not a particularly positive one, was the new pop music of the decade and the young people who acquired vast wealth and fame through making it, especially The Beatles and The Rolling Stones. As the music and the lifestyles became more radical and adventurous, my mother became more and more indignant, and heated and rancorous arguments raged in the house in the forest lit by paraffin lamps between my brother and my mother. In winter at least, the four of us spent most of our time after dark or in bad weather in the long, narrow kitchen and living room that was the only room that we could continuously keep well lit and heated. This was the place for listening to the radio and for conversation and argument, and all four of us heard the same thing whether we liked it or not. I have a vivid memory of that room made up of countless evenings and nights. The wind is howling in the chimney and in the roof, the whole room looks rather like the forecastle of an old wooden sailing ship afloat on the black sea of the valley in darkness, and my brother and mother are arguing, arguing about pop music and the behaviour of the idols of younger generation. I have always enjoyed discussion, argument and debate, but perhaps because of what I heard in those cramped conditions, I have always disliked letting emotion get into discussions – I dislike it when I fall into it myself and I dislike it when others do it. There is a maxim attributed to Lenin that I am fond of: *The heart on fire and the brain on ice.* A little more ice would have been appropriate on those long evenings in our home.

My mother and father were reclusive people and they did not travel, nor did my mother work outside the home until I was almost twelve years old, and so there was much in that decade that irritated her, and no doubt the seclusion of where we lived added to her suspicions. She disapproved of the young women in increasingly short miniskirts who came walking in the valley with their boyfriends on summer days, or sat opposite us with their boyfriends on the red Number 8 bus travelling into Swansea. In her eyes, girls should be able to dress glamorously without showing – or running the risk of showing – their knickers.

Stories about space travel and life on other planets have been about for centuries, but only in the 1960s did space travel become a reality. At Christmas 1965 I was given a battery-operated Dalek and a space rocket powered by rubber bands. I do remember that on clear nights in the valley the stars and planets were amazingly bright, today of course, we would call the valley a dark site, an increasingly rare oasis away from light pollution, and perhaps my own love of astronomy began at that time. I don't think my parents had much respect for the attempts to put human beings on the moon or for science in general, and my own respect for science grew as a reaction against their attitude. My mother changed her mind about this in later years. We were all to change our minds about a great deal after that astonishing decade.

SUMMER

This season was saturated by colour and better for the elaborate games of the imagination. Bursts of magenta, pink and scarlet flared in the dark greens of the woodland in early summer where the rhododendrons stood, while the air was always heavy with the drone of insects and the smell of blossoms whenever the sun shone from June to September. When I found my way into the Walled Gardens, the stillness throbbed secretively. Snakes appeared in summer, and among them the adder or viper did carry some amount of risk for a child. In the Old Quarry, so overgrown that it looked like a natural woodland ravine, I once came across a large snake, speckled and bronze, rearing out of last year's dry leaves. It was only a harmless grass snake, but its sudden appearance startled me so much that I leapt back and rolled down a sharp slope beside me. In summer I was not driven indoors by the cold or forced to keep moving, and in school holidays I was frequently out from early morning until late evening. The bright plastics and shiny golds and silvers of toy weapons and the smell of the smoke of cap guns were all more intense, more intoxicating in the warmth and sunshine. I lived in a world of Western gunfights, Indian raids, pirate battles, cavalry charges that came from the pages of comics and comic book annuals and from visits to the cinema in Swansea (all the more sharply engraved on my imagination because I never watched television), all shading off effortlessly into the forests and fields around me. I played alone with figures from my imagination.

Even later, after the age of nine or ten when I became more popular in school and boys came on their bikes to play with me, this usually happened only in summer. These visits are bound up with the smells of wet shoes, wet jeans, warm lemonade, boys sweating after running. They called me Woodcutter in school, so I led them into the deepest, darkest parts of the valley and frightened them with stories of prowlers and werewolves.

There were days when I did not play alone or with other boys because I was with my father. Every so often in summer, despite his bad health, he decided to do quite boyish things. He had retired from work at sixty-two because of the state his chest, not at sixty-five, as was normal with industrial workers and after retirement he occupied himself with the endless need for firewood or the heavier supplies such as paraffin from the village.

'Go and ask your mother for some bacon.' My father was sitting on an upturned milk crate, with his back against the wall of the house, smoking his pipe thoughtfully.

'Raw bacon?' I asked.

'Yes. Ask her to wrap it up. And bring the rest of that flagon of cider, it's about half full, and a drink for yourself. Put them all in that old haversack I used to take to work.'

This sounded too interesting to miss, so I ran into the house before he could change his mind. Despite the almost violent, glaring heat of the day, my mother had decided to bake some kind of pie, so that her face was bright pink with the heat of the kitchen and smudged with flour. She was also very short on patience and muttered as she wrapped the bacon in greaseproof paper and thrust it at me without asking any questions. I found the haversack and slipped off into our large pantry, shadowy and the size of a small room, where I picked up the cider and some homemade ginger beer for myself. As I ran into the sunlight again I did not give a single thought to my hot and overworked mother, after all, I was nine years old, dedicated to my own enjoyment and to celebrating the summer. Also, this scheme was my father's idea from the first, although I was often quite capable of helping myself to food from the pantry without asking first and setting off on my own crazy expeditions.

My father now shouldered the haversack and Prince, our German shepherd, quickly got up and left the patch of deep shade in which he was lying and followed us, with my dog Tim, the brown and white mongrel behind him. We set off down through the birches in the direction of the river, and I either ran ahead of my father or bounced along at his side, full of a sense of conspiracy and adventure. Our home was, of course, a matriarchy dominated by my mother and because of this I had a rather spiteful sense of elation that was bound up with being in alliance with my father and escaping my mother's authority.

We followed the path through the ferns and down a steep bank on which an oak tree stood and into a natural hollow at the bottom of the slope. Away to the left was a huge expanse of bamboos humming with insects in the heat, one of the many kinds of exotic plant that had run wild in the valley. There was plenty of dead wood around and I brought armfuls of it to my father while he built and lit a fire, then we sat on mossy outcrops at the foot of the slope and stared at the blaze. The flames seemed fiercer in the bright sunlight, for some reason, than the flames of similar fires we had made after dark. The wood was so dry that in a very short time it had burnt down to red-hot embers, and my father stood up and took a rolled up square of wire mesh from the pocket of his jacket and slowly unwound it. Next, he cut four notched sticks with his knife and sharpened them and stuck them into the ground around the fire, stretching the wire mesh between them, low over the embers.

'Bring that bacon, then, boy.'

The rashers were broad and thick and they soon began to hiss and frizzle on the wire mesh, and soon my father looked at them with a sort of fixed seriousness and turned them over with another sharpened stick, then he handed me his knife.

'Cut yourself a sharp stick to take your bacon with.'

That knife always fascinated me, partly because it was old, the black handle polished with age, the steel of the square-tipped blade stained dark with years of use. When I took the bacon, it was hot enough to hurt my fingers, even when holding it at the very edge of the rind, but of course, I didn't let that show and pretended my hands were as toughened as those of my father. My mother always cooked a large breakfast and had done so today, but we hadn't cooked and eaten the bacon because we needed it but because doing so was its own justification and reward, and the pleasure in it was ceremonial. My father now drank some cider and I drank some ginger beer while he lit his pipe. The dogs, sitting expectantly a little distance away, were rewarded by having some bacon rinds hurled in their direction.

'Is it true that a man hanged himself in the valley?' I asked my father.

'Who told you that?'

'I heard you talking about it once.' I leaned back and swigged more ginger beer.

'Aye, it's true.' My father pushed some of the smouldering embers into the fire with the tip of his heavy boot.

'Where did he hang himself?'

'Quite a way down beyond Middle Lodge.'
'Did you find him?'

My father relit his pipe and puffed on it in the way that so prolongs conversations with pipe smokers, staring at the remains of the fire as he did so.

'No, I didn't find him. He was found by a man out shooting, or out walking, as I recall. I was nearby and the man who found him came to fetch me.'

'So you saw him? You saw the man who had hanged himself?'
'Yes.'
'What was it like?'
'I don't wish to speak of it. It's too horrible.'
'Why did he kill himself?'
'I understand he was very unhappy, I suppose he couldn't see any other way out of his trouble.'

It was my turn to fall silent and stare at the fire now. I knew that people were sometimes killed, because I loved adventure stories. Also, I knew that very old people died, like Sir John Dillwyn Llewelyn, and that very ill people died. Despite all that, for a boy of nine on a day in summer to imagine how someone could be so unhappy that he killed himself was impossible. I accepted it as true, because my father had told me, but I could not feel it to be true.

The fire had turned to a few glowing fragments, the glow barely visible in the strong sunlight, with white ash blown by the occasional breeze, and so my father put some stones and lumps of earth on it, then picked up the haversack again. We walked on past the bamboos and into the forest where the trees pressed closer together and the green shade was very deep, on and on, through the little clearing where the ground was boggy and the wild watercress, that we sometimes picked for Sunday tea, grew in the shadows. After more thick woodland, we came out again on the bank of the river Llan, a very little river, hardly more than a stream. Despite the present hot weather, there had been heavy rain some weeks ago and so the river was quite full. We stood silently surveying the deep, dark water immediately below the bank and the stony shallows further down stream where the fractured sunlight played and glittered.

Prince, the German shepherd came to sniff at the lush grass right on the edge of the bank. On a sudden, unkind impulse, I pushed him violently into the river putting my whole weight and strength into hurling myself against his black back and tawny side, then shrieking with laughter. He went under, surfaced, and swam into the shallows, looking supremely unconcerned, soon joined by Tim the mongrel. My mother would have told me off for treating a dog with such disrespect, but my father made no comment, merely taking out his pipe again and smoking. He seemed to be thinking something over and presently he took one of my mother's nylon stockings from the pocket of his jacket and threaded a length of wire in a hoop through the top of the stocking to keep it open, and then fixed the whole thing to a stick he cut from a bush behind us. I sat on the edge of the bank with my legs swinging and watched him as he took off his boots and socks and rolled up the legs of his trousers and waded out into the river with his homemade net. There were indeed fish in the river at that time, but if my father really expected to catch any in this way he must have been either the World's Best Fisherman or the World's Worst Fisherman and Greatest Optimist. He was in the river a long time and I sat watching him and whittling a stick with his knife. At last, he tired of this pastime and no doubt felt the cold getting into his ankles and waded back to the bank.

'What's poetry?' I asked rather irrelevantly as he was putting his boots and socks back on.

'Well...It's...Poetry is like a song or a nursery rhyme when it's written down. People write it when they want to say something in a prettier way.'

'Can you write poetry?' I demanded idly, expecting my father to say that of course he couldn't and that only brilliantly clever people could do such a thing, but instead he sat gazing at the river and considering.

'Yes I can. I could write a poem.'

'I bet you can't!'

'I can.' He sounded a little irritable and he was probably searching for some feat to make up for his failure to catch a fish. To my surprise, he searched in his jacket and came up with the wrapper from an ounce of tobacco which he turned blank side upwards, then he found a pencil that he sometimes used to write down the football results he heard on the radio, and finally he filled and lit his pipe again. There was a very, very long silence during which he frowned and squinted through the smoke of his pipe and stared at the river more than he wrote. Finally, with an air of considerable triumph, he handed me the result.

'Oh for a bound right out of town,
To sit by the stream that bubbles drowns,
To look at the dark and trout-filled pool
Where the bright-finned fish flit about like fools,
To breathe the pure air that clears the head,
To take healthy exercise that sends you gladly to bed.'

by Jack Edgar James

Being nine years old, I was speechless with admiration and stared at him as if he had performed some magic that defied the laws of nature. It was all very well to see this kind of stuff in books in school, but it was quite different to see my father just take out a pencil and write it! Until then, my father had impressed me only with his stubbornness, physical strength, knowledge of football (which did not interest me at all) and his apparent complete inability to be afraid of anything, even when faced with three aggressive young men, fifty years younger than himself and carrying loaded shotguns. Now he had written a poem! So there it was, my father's first and only literary work – at least to the best of my knowledge. I kept the piece of paper well into adult life and came to know the lines off by heart, though he never gave it a title.

At some time in my early childhood, Mr Thomas and his brother of Bryndafydd Farm began to use the broad, curving field that started on the other side of the garden fence of Upper Lodge. It was a magical thing to me to see the plough behind their red tractor turn the stubbled ground into glistening chocolate brown furrows. I liked Mr Malcolm Thomas best, because he occasionally let me ride on the tractor on a bitter winter day and look back in the vibrating roar and see the earth opening behind us, with the seagulls swooping and circling over the ground, their cries hardly audible over the noise of the tractor. In the weeks leading up to Christmas, there were sometimes beef cattle in the field, chased by my dog Tim, until they bunched together and stampeded after him as he effortlessly kept just out of their way and I whooped with laughter. If Malcolm ever saw this, he kindly ignored it. When there was nothing but short stubble in the field in the late summer, my brother John and I played cricket there, using an oil drum as a wicket. Being nine years older than me, my brother was only interested in playing sporting games with me.

The hay baling began on the day after my father's failure at fishing and his success with verse. I had been waiting for this for days while the cut hay lay turning tawny yellow and dry on the ground. The noise of the baling machine was so loud that I could hear it in the quiet of the valley when it was still a very long way from the house. The baling machine pulled by the tractor was a grimy blue and had some kind of mechanism on its back that looked to me like twin hammers rising and falling by turns. The noise it made was like steady, repeated gunshots, while from its rear end, like some grotesque mechanical hen laying rectangular eggs, the hay bales were pushed out and fell onto the ground. I ran beside the tractor, shouting and waving at Malcolm, then jumped onto the hay bales and from one bale straight onto another if the machine dropped them close enough together. At that age I was not strong enough to lift a hay bale, but I could push and roll them, and when I ran out of wind from running I made myself a den out several hay bales shoved together. Malcolm circled that huge field in the glaring heat, in circuits that gradually grew smaller. When all the field was done, he told me to push as many of the bales as I could away from the edge of the field and further in towards the centre, ready for the trailer that would come to collect them in two or three hours. Whether or not this made any difference to the work, Malcolm knew children well enough to realise that I would take enormous pride in carrying out the task. He drove away now, and all was quiet again.

I worked until I felt nauseous with mild heatstroke and went to lie in the grass under an oak tree near the house. My mother finally called me and told me to come in and have something to eat and drink, but all the while I listened tensely for the sound of the tractor and trailer.

At last, Malcolm and all his family reappeared. In the traditional way, some of the young men from the village had turned out to help load up the hay bales. They thrust pitchforks into them and swung them up onto the trailer, sweating profusely, showing a strength that I could only envy. But at least I could ride on the trailer, rolling some of the bales into a better position and chattering self-importantly to Malcolm. The load grew taller and the swaying increased and I listened curiously to the talk.

'Can't you lift better than that, boy? That Old Inn bitter is ruining you.'

'I'll be lifting hay bales or pints long after you're flat on your face.'

'Where's Kevin?'

'Broke his ankle playing football with his kids. You won't see him today. Watch out! This is a heavy one.'

They may well have toned down their language of their own accord because of my presence, and perhaps because Malcolm would not have tolerated bad language in front of a child, so that what I heard was surprisingly mild.

There was another tractor and trailer in the field now and another party of men helping, and I sometimes ran between the two trailers. When the hay bales were all loaded I rode on top of one of the trailers as it swayed towards the village, with the mosquitoes already tormenting our faces. They set me down at Home Farm and I ran home in the sudden, resounding quiet, with the brassy light turning to mauves and greys.

Today, that huge field lies under an extensive housing estate. Would I have believed that such a thing could happen at nine years old? Yes, I think I would have believed it, even then – but not on that particular day.

WINTER

This was the season that intensified the isolation of the valley and our home because there were fewer people about and because the weather and the darkness kept us indoors much more. I remember returning home one Saturday evening about a week before Christmas, after shopping in Swansea. My father and I had gone ahead and my mother and brother were some way behind. We were at a point on the drive where the slope climbed steeply on our right, trees overhung us, and other massive trees growing out of the side of the valley screened everything to our left. The bitter frost and the complete darkness and the overwhelming silence were intense, so intense that I felt a dull ache pass through my heart, although I was not normally nervous in the forest or in the darkness. It was the first time that I fully realised how utterly remote our home could be. There was no motorway to the north of the valley in those days, no distant roar of traffic and far fewer vehicles generally. Icy silence and darkness. I had a child's vague sense of how small and fragile even a grown man like my father was in a winter landscape. Later on, at bedtime, the Aladdin lamp was blown out, the candles were blown out, and in my bed I remembered with dread that numbing solitude and freezing darkness outside the house.

In our home it was the custom to cut down and decorate the Christmas tree on Christmas Eve itself – there was certainly no shortage of trees to choose from. As we had no electricity, we did not have decorations that lit up, only coloured glass balls and tinsel. Ornamental candles were clipped onto the tree but my parents would not allow them to be lit in case of accidental fire. The Christmas puddings cooked by my mother weeks before began to be eaten that evening. Year after year, I was so excited on the night before Christmas Day that I hardly slept at all. At Christmas 1963 I was given a large toy Winchester rifle, in 1964 a battery operated tractor, in 1965 a battery operated Dalek, in 1966 an Action Man. The vividness of the impression these things left on my mind can be seen in how clearly I remember them after more than forty years. Perhaps the complete absence of other children and of people in general made Christmas more intense for me. Other members of the family, such as there were, never stayed with us over Christmas.

On Christmas morning, when I could at last unwrap my presents, I was in a frenzy of excitement, and eventually my mother almost had to physically force me to eat some breakfast, although I was only too eager to eat anything else. There were chocolates, dates and figs. Nuts always came in their shells in those days and were broken open with the iron that my mother heated up in the oven to iron my shirts for school or with my father's hammer, placing the nuts on the tiled surround of the grate. I had cried with pain more than once on Christmas morning after hitting my thumb as I opened nuts, and I usually pestered the adults repeatedly to open them for me. There seemed to be an endless supply of small cans of orangeade, lemonade and limeade that lacked the pull-off tabs of later years and needed to be punctured in two places with a can opener. Both my father and my brother smoked, and on Christmas Day they would smoke cigars, so that the smell of cigar smoke is always bound up with childhood Christmases for me. The long kitchen and living room soon grew steamy with cooking as the fire was stoked up with wood, or some years with coal left at North Lodge and carried to our house on my father's cart. I remember looking on with fascinated horror on Christmas Eve as my mother prepared a whole goose for cooking, or a whole duck another year. As a child, I never enjoyed my Christmas dinner any the less for watching this gruesome spectacle, although in adulthood I have become a vegetarian.

We always had bunches of balloons hanging from the ceiling and these would sometimes suddenly burst in the rising heat or break loose and float down onto the fire, the paraffin stove or the two rings of the gas cooker that worked off a pressurised cylinder. Christmas crackers came in solid, opaque cardboard boxes and had a far less glossy feel than they have nowadays. In the background, the radio always played, carols, comedy shows, news, the Queen's broadcast, when anything could be heard over the noise of the games I played with my toys. I was forbidden to eat anything for the two hours before Christmas dinner was served, even the small tangerines that were bought at Christmas time, each individually wrapped in pretty paper in those days. It was during those two hours that I went out for a walk, sometimes with my father, but more often with my brother, or alone, as my father stayed indoors as much as possible in the winter because of his chest. Even the dogs, running along with us, seemed affected by the excitement, and seemed to sense that special feel in the air, that special look to the sky that was present on no other day in the year. It was tacitly understood that I got out of my mother's way as the cooking, never easy in those conditions, reached its most stressful stage. I usually returned just as the goose, duck or turkey had finally been roasted to my mother's satisfaction in the oven beside the fire.

Christmas dinners were always huge, and my parents, who normally did not drink in the house, would go as far as taking a glass of port or sherry with the meal. My mother also sometimes made her own elderberry wine, strong and dark red. It took a great deal of nagging and pleading for me to be allowed a small sip of port or sherry, which I quite liked, but much less begging to be given a glass of elderberry wine, somehow this was not quite counted as alcohol, though it was quite strong stuff. The only other time that alcoholic drinks appeared in the house was when an occasional flagon of cider was bought at the height of summer. Unfortunately for me, I didn't like the elderberry wine much because it was far too dry for my taste. Many years later, I lived in rural Spain where it is normal for all children to be given wine diluted with water at mealtimes.

I was always hungry enough to eat all my Christmas dinner, and afterwards the endless playing with presents, pulling crackers, eating Christmas snacks continued, either in the house or outside, according to the weather and the nature of the presents I had been given. Outside the house, the valley was steeped in a deep, contemplative quietness that was special to Christmas. Sadly, Christmas Day was not really endless at all and all too soon the short December day slipped into dusk and darkness and the winter night stretched everywhere around our long, narrow room with its hazy lamplight catching on the decorated tree. I was still engrossed in my presents and in quieter moments I would read, or someone would read to me. In the background there was some programme on the radio that I found inexpressibly boring, but there were two exceptions. The Dickens story *A Christmas Carol* and *Memories of Christmas* by Dylan Thomas were sometimes broadcast in those days, and although the humour in them is very adult, I enjoyed and appreciated both from a young age.

The harsh winter of 1962-63 was the only time I can remember when there were other children living in the valley. Linda Williams was about my age and she and her sisters had come to live in Middle Lodge in summer 1961, but I had nothing to do with the girls for over a year after this because of my awkwardness with other children, of whom I had no experience, and because they were girls. The conventions of childhood in the early sixties somehow filtered through to me at some level even before I started school, which meant that I sensed that only boys who were sissies kept company with girls. By the time of that severe winter in early 1963 I saw a good deal of Linda in school and secretly I liked her very much. However, my friend Tony Gilbank and I felt obliged to act like boys, and so we followed Linda around in the playground, making silly noises to annoy her and interrupt her games with other girls, or else we ignored her altogether.

The water supply to Middle Lodge was piped from a well south of the house, deep in the woods, and pipes extended on northwards to Upper Lodge. Even as far back as that winter, the pipes ceased to work in severe weather, though fortunately all of the various inhabitants of Middle Lodge, in the spirit of remote rural places, were always more than willing for us to take our water from the tap in their kitchen. Linda's parents were also very welcoming to us each time we needed to call for water. I remember arriving with my father, who was pushing his handcart, on a dark evening that was in the grip of the biting frost. The cart was loaded with two crates of washed out pop bottles for drinking water and a scrubbed out milk churn that provided a larger supply of water. We also had a large water tank near our house that collected rainwater.

Linda and her sisters, Mair and Helen, were outside the house, so I began making the same kind of silly noises I made in the playground in school, just to annoy her.
'Don't start that!' Linda said ferociously. I was suddenly aware that I was on my own, with Tony Gilbank far away, and that Linda had her sisters to back her up. In any case, my father called me away to come and help. I was far too small to help carry the milk churn when it was full of water, but I could help my father carry the metal milk crates of water bottles. The ground was icy in places and the metal crates seemed to burn into my hands if I took my mittens off. My father's gloved hands slipped on the wet churn as he struggled

with it and he coughed and coughed again, his mouth muffled by the blue woollen scarf that my mother had knitted for him.

The winter grew steadily worse after this, there was snow and more snow, and we heard of drivers trapped in lorries in blizzard conditions when we listened to the evening news on the radio. I did not go to school for some weeks, sometimes because I was ill, sometimes because of the freak weather. The well supplying Middle Lodge froze at times, and if we did not have enough water, we went to the river, a much longer trip over much worse ground, though not as far away from us as the lake.

The lake eventually froze too, and I went there with my brother and Prince the German shepherd, watching in wonder as the dog walked out on the solid surface of water he had been swimming in, just a few months before. My brother would not let me walk out onto the ice, no doubt foreseeing that he would get the blame if the ice gave way and I disappeared, but he went some distance out on it himself. In childhood so many things are seen for the first time, in this case the extraordinary fact that water can freeze hard enough to walk on. About that time, we heard that a teenage boy had broken through the ice with a metal bar and then slipped into the hole. He was bravely rescued from death by drowning and hypothermia by Linda's father, who dragged him out and called an ambulance.

The snow was very deep in Swede's Field one day and my brother and I began to roll a snowball across the ground so that it picked up more and more snow and grew larger and larger. The thing grew so large that we could not move it any further, even by our combined strength, and we left it at the side of the field. Naturally, this monstrous snowball froze hard on successive nights of frost, so that it remained there without melting for about two weeks after all the other snow had gone and the days began to grow mild and sunny. Resentfully, I had to go to school more often as that savage winter drew to an end, but I kept going to the field to see whether the giant snowball was quite gone because it seemed my link with the severe weather (which I hoped would return) and with the freedom of the cold spell.

It was not only the weather that was cruel. I was going shopping with my mother one day towards the end of the winter, walking the long drive up into the village as we always had to, noticing the patches of snow that still clung in sheltered places. We had already passed the site of the demolished big house when we heard an appalling shrieking coming from the bushes beside the track. We stopped and stared at a rabbit on a patch of snow, twitching and jerking in its death throes and shrieking horribly, with a weasel striking and striking at its neck. The weasel became aware of us and – grudgingly and malevolently, it seemed – backed away further into the dry leaves. There was nothing to be done, as the rabbit was almost dead. As soon as we began to walk on, the weasel came forward and began dragging the rabbit in an amazing manifestation of ferocity and strength. In reality, animals only follow their natural course like the seasons, and it is only human beings who are truly capable of cruelty.

LITERATURE AND LAMPLIGHT

It is a hot Sunday afternoon, but cool as always in the house, with a great stillness inside the sandstone walls and outside in the valley, and my mother is reading to me in my bedroom as she often did. The book is *She* by H. Rider Haggard, a book that caught my imagination and fascinated me at the time. Outside in the summer heat was a forest with far more exotic and tropical trees and plants than can usually be found growing wild in Britain, as well as secretive, crumbling ruins, walls rearing up in woodland clearings, worn and mossy stone steps climbing up wooded slopes. *She* is, of course, the story of She Who Must Be Obeyed, Ayesha, the white sorceress who rules a remote African race. As I have said, my own home was certainly a matriarchy, and as well as this, my mother's only close friend, Mrs Nozicka of North Lodge was an exceptionally strong personality, fiercely outspoken, kind, proud and willing to stand up to all comers. In my last two years at the village primary school I was taught by Miss Christine Hedges, decent, compassionate, but incredibly strict and domineering, a teacher who pushed and pushed and pushed us to work, work, work, as well as giving generously of her own time and energy to teach us handicrafts. Rider Haggard's novel meshed easily with the landscape of my childhood and with the dynamics of social life in my world. I was used to strong women who commanded respect, and I recall that by far the brightest pupil and the hardest worker in my age group at primary school was a girl called Anne.

I cannot say that I think so very highly of *She* now, but at one point in my childhood it seemed half parable of my life in the valley, half description of it. I was a bright child and a solitary one, and I lacked the distractions of television and an urban environment, so that it was pretty inevitable that I would live much of my time in the world of books. The Penllergare Valley Woods shaped my taste in books, just as it has shaped many aspects of my outlook on the world. I have strong feelings about what is now called the developing world in which a shortage of water and the need to carry water over long distances is a problem for millions of people – a problem of which I had personal experience until the age of twelve.

Before I went to school at the age of five, when I was at home in the daytime with my mother, there were programmes for schools on the radio, and at that very young age, the dramatisation of myths, mainly Norse and Greek myths, gripped me more than anything else. Perhaps they seemed more interesting and real to me because I stepped out of our house into a forested valley, rather than into a modern housing estate or a street in a town.

Next came Kenneth Grahame's *The Wind in the Willows*. I cannot remember a single week going by when I was not looking at the pictures in this book, or having it read to me (it was an unabridged edition and some of the more difficult words and passages may have been skipped when I was very young, though not many.) As with other books, *The Wind in the Willows* seemed almost a description of my everyday reality. I only had to go outside and there it all was – or at least most of it. There was a river, a river bank, and there was certainly a Wild Wood, frightening at dusk on winter nights when there were unexplained noises in the dry leaves. In Kenneth Grahame's story the countryside is idealised and idyllic, but that was mainly how I regarded the valley, for me it *was* idyllic, because of the irresponsibility of childhood I was largely immune to the hardships and anxieties of our life, and even the toughest aspects seemed a kind of game to me most of the time. Even my father, in summer at least, sometimes fell into Ratty's attitude that the main point of each day is to indulge in boyish pastimes. There is also the obsession with the enjoyment of food that Kenneth Grahame shares with Dickens, often to be eaten in the open air, and this was something else that I was used to, because thanks to my mother we always ate well. I had an enormous amount of toys and books of all kinds, considering that we were not at all well off, something that encouraged a Toad of Toad Hall attitude to life as a long succession of crazes and pastimes, the latest being discarded to take up the next one.

Above all, the Wild Wood in which Badger lives has grown upon the site of an old Roman town. The following passage from *The Wind in the Willows* was quoted by Gavin Weightman in his book *Brave New Wilderness*, and it comes from the chapter in which the Mole is being shown around Badger's huge underground home. It is a passage that might almost have been written about Penllergare Valley Woods, the lost estate of the Dillwyn Llewelyn family. I dimly recognised the parallel even in childhood.

'How on earth Badger,' he said at last, 'did you ever find time and strength to do all this? It's astonishing.'
'It would be astonishing indeed,' said the Badger simply, 'if I had done it. But as a matter of fact I did none of it – only cleaned out the passages and chambers, as far as I had need of them. There's a lot more of it, all round about. I see you don't understand, and I must explain it to you. Well, very long ago, on the spot where the Wild Wood waves now, before ever it had planted itself and grown up to what it now is, there was a city – a city of people, you know. Here where we are standing they lived, and walked and talked and slept and carried on their business. Here they stabled their horses and feasted, from here they rode out to fight or drove out to trade. They were powerful people, and rich and great builders. They built to last for they thought their city would last forever.'
'But what has become of them all?' asked the Mole.
'Who can tell?' said the Badger. 'People come – they stay for a while, they flourish, they build – and they go. It is their way. But we remain. There were badgers here, I've been told, long before that city ever came to be. And now there are badgers here again. We are an enduring lot, and we may move out for a time, but we wait, and are patient, and back we come. And so it will ever be.'

I went through a King Arthur and His Knights phase, my surroundings were favourable to it! It lasted far longer than the three weeks or so during which I was read a chapter each evening from the battered, red hardback edition of an abridgement of Malory's *Le Morte d'Arthur*. The plastic sword in a plastic scabbard were easy, as for lance and a shield, I used a metal bar that was once part of a fence and the square metal sheet with a handle fixed in the centre that was placed in front of the fire to make the fire burn up more quickly and then removed. (My wife tells me this is called a blazer, but my mother called it a blower.) *Treasure Island* also made an immense impression on me, as it did upon my own daughter when I read it to her in her own childhood. Admittedly, the valley was very far from the sea, but most of the action of the book takes place on the desert island (the tropical and exotic vegetation came in handy once again!) There is also the fact that Jim Hawkins is a lone boy in a world of adults. At night, in bed, I terrified myself with the idea that Blind Pew would come down the drive, tapping his way with his stick, perhaps this was not completely due to my overheated imagination, as some strange individuals did occasionally wander in to the valley.

Stories of the Old American West came to me through comic books, weekly comics and comic book annuals, and also, my father was addicted to cheap paperback Westerns, although these were not the only books he read. Western stories gripped my imagination more powerfully and for a longer time than any other kind of reading in the first ten years of my life, and the psychological reasons for this are not hard to find. The Penllergare Valley was the Wild West, the frontier, pioneer country, and that was where I lived, but the children who went to school with me lived in modern houses in normal streets in the village, and so they lived 'back east' as the characters in cowboy stories describe it. The village and Swansea were the industrialised world where life was soft and easy, so that once again my reading and my games reflected – and came close to describing in my childhood mind – the actual realities of my life. In the cheap Wild West fiction of those days, the Native Americans were almost always the villains, but I was almost invariably on their side. I decided that like myself they lived in wild places and were misunderstood and were not welcome when they went to towns and settlements. Despite the good influences of Miss Thomas in the admission class, Miss Hedges in my last two years in primary school, and my friend Tony Gilbank, I never settled well at school and was not happy there.

The Native Americans also lived with the constant threat of their wilderness home being encroached upon and tamed, a fate rather similar to that which threatened the valley throughout my childhood and later. In Westerns, the cowboys, gunfighters and scouts are also sturdy loners, something that appeals to a solitary child playing make-believe games alone. The cinema also fed my passion for Westerns on the occasions when we went to see films, about once every six weeks or so, as I recall. My brother took me to see *The Magnificent Seven* when I was about eight, three or four years after it was first released, although this film is of course a cinema classic loved by people who otherwise dislike Westerns. The sixties were still great years for Western films, at least of the popular kind, and even the cheapest of them burned deeply into my imagination because I saw films so infrequently, so that I would act out scenes from them for days afterwards. There was one other reading experience that I came to because of my father's and my own passion for Westerns. As I began to read more and more, he recommended a book called *Cimarron* by Edna Ferber, though I did not sit down to read it until I was almost twelve. This, however, is no typical cowboy adventure story, instead it describes the struggles of a young woman in Oklahoma in the late nineteenth century, deserted by her husband and fighting against poverty and harsh conditions – yet another strong heroine! Curiously, *Cimarron* and Edna Ferber seem to have been unfairly forgotten today.

There was a library in the room used by the class taught by Miss Hedges, and we were allowed, indeed encouraged, to borrow books and take them home, as long as we checked with her first. It was here that I found an abridged but beautifully illustrated edition of James Fenimore Cooper's *The Last of the Mohicans*, a book that treated the Native Americans far more sympathetically than anything I had read before that time. Most of the story is set in the forests, near rivers, lakes and waterfalls, and as well as this, both Hawkeye and Chingachgook the Mohican are outsiders, at odds with their own societies. Miss Hedges might not have approved if she knew how much I rushed and skipped my homework in order to hurry off down to the banks of the Llan in the early summer of 1967, carrying a real sheath-knife and a toy gun, in order to turn the valley into Cooper's wilderness. The games were only made uncomfortable by the mosquitoes that grew active towards twilight so near to the river. The class library also yielded a biography of Davy Crockett (no doubt much idealised) the congressman from the backwoods and hero of the Alamo. For some reason, this book was read with interest by my mother and brother as well as by my father.

One afternoon, as a break from working hard, Miss Hedges read to us from a book of animal stories. The story was actually a chapter from Jack London's *White Fang*. There was a pause.

'I think this is a horrible part of the story.' Miss Hedges warned us and went on to read the description of White Fang as a cub eating ptarmigan chicks. Having grown up with two dogs in the valley woods, the episode didn't seem especially horrible to me, particularly as our huge German shepherd was rather wolfish. More important, I was spellbound by Jack London's writing and relieved to find that there was a copy of *White Fang* in the class library, and I immediately borrowed it and read it, then read it again – devoured it would be a better description.

I remember Miss Hedges as a lady with reddish blonde hair and a generous figure, always full of energy and enthusiasm. Although, as I have said, she maintained strict discipline and worked us very hard, she was also extremely kind and made learning fun. She never smacked or slapped any of us, or punished us physically in any way, though this was still a common practice in those days. Very occasionally, she would joke about putting some of the more badly behaved boys over her knee, including me. For the most part, I joined in with the other boys in insulting Miss Hedges behind her back and calling her names, but secretly I adored her and found it painful to leave her when I went to the grammar school. Although I almost came to blows with some of the boys on one occasion and defended Miss Hedges as 'the best teacher in the school', I think almost every one of her pupils – whether boys or girls – were deeply fond of her. I never integrated well in school and did not go to university until I was thirty-one, as a mature student, so that Miss Hedges and Miss Thomas of the admission class were the only teachers for whom I felt any affection, whether in primary school or in grammar school. Strangely, perhaps, these teachers came into my life during the years I lived in the valley woods, and it may have been that the isolation and remoteness of my home increased my appreciation of adults I could respect.

Most of the heroes of Jack London's books, whether they are human beings or dogs, are sturdy and self-sufficient loners, and his novels and stories tend to be set in wild places where hardship and deprivation are usual. From *White Fang*, I went to *The Call of the Wild* and *The Sea Wolf*, and my appetite for his books was insatiable, especially as the quality of my own life grew harsher around the age of twelve. Apart from the main titles, most of his books were out of print (he wrote about fifty in total.) Fortunately, at about this time, I discovered Ralph's Second-Hand Bookshop in Swansea, still owned and run at that time by Mr Ralph Wishart, once a friend of Dylan Thomas. By the age of eleven I was travelling on the red double-decker bus, the number 8, on lone expeditions to Ralph's, spending all my money on battered copies of Jack London's books. There were some of his novels, especially the political ones, that I did not properly understand for another two or three years, but most of his books meshed with my childhood experiences and my surroundings as well, or better than, anything I read in those years.

At about the same age, I began to read Dylan Thomas, or his stories at least, and felt an extraordinary sense of exhilaration – this writer was describing things I thought only I had experienced. At first sight, there would seem to be little similarity between my childhood in the Penllergare Valley Woods and the boyhood of Dylan Thomas, an English teacher's son who grew up in Cwmdonkin Drive in a middle class area of Swansea. However, the early stories in *Portrait of the Artist as a Young Dog*, as well as some of the best of the radio broadcasts are concerned with visits to relatives in rural areas, who were individuals as eccentric as my own family. Dylan Thomas also has an unusual gift for conveying the moment-to-moment sensations of childhood.

In the autumn of 1968, when I had just turned twelve, I discovered Tolkien's *The Lord of the Rings*, and I was to read that huge book three times before I was fourteen. As with the other books that meant so much to me in childhood, I would not have responded so intensely to Tolkien if I had not grown up in the valley, and for a time this author rivalled and even ousted Jack London. Tolkien's world is pre-industrial, except of course for Mordor, the evil empire. As I was unhappy at school, a shy and rather reclusive boy in a boys' grammar school, I increasingly had reason to think of the valley woods as a refuge and the urban world beyond as threatening, and I was also, like Frodo, on a journey into dangerous and unknown territory – the territory of puberty and adolescence. As well as these difficulties, I knew quite well that our life in the valley was coming to an end and I used *The Lord of the Rings* as a sort of psychological shield, and sometimes as a literal, physical shield as well. The thick paperback book with its yellow spine travelled with me to school in my satchel and I opened it and read it at every available opportunity. The older boys teased me and the teachers grew angry.

'Are you just pretending to read that book? Why don't you skip a few hundred pages and read the end? Shall I read the end to you?'

'James! Put that wretched book away and pay attention! If I see it again I shall confiscate it.'

Oh well! Teachers and older boys were very similar to goblins, trolls and orcs! At the end of the day I would go home to the valley woods (the Shire, Rivendell, Gondor – one of the good places in the story.)

Like Tolkien's world of Middle Earth, the valley was always being threatened with being swallowed up by the industrialised world, and like Middle Earth it contained many crumbling and mysterious ruins that were the relics of past grandeur.

In 1968, *The Lord of the Rings* was not yet so generally famous and known to almost everyone, and as I was already considered odd, reading such a huge book on such a strange subject made me stand out as even more odd. There was one other reason for the book's appeal for me and that was its mental atmosphere. It is often forgotten today that most of the book was written during the Second World War and that Tolkien was a Roman Catholic, so that the war against Nazi Germany and the general perception of life as a battlefield on which the forces of good and evil fight each other feeds into the atmosphere of the tale. My parents were not Catholics, but my mother was a convinced Christian, and as I have said before, the war was a crucial experience in the lives of my parents, so that I was brought up on memories of the war.

Would I have been gripped by J. K. Rowling's *Harry Potter* novels if they had been available to me in my childhood? I think not, though I admire them as an adult, having been introduced to them by my daughter. I think I would have been put off by the school setting, by the urban setting of much of the action, by Harry's eagerness to return to school at the end of each summer holiday, by the difficulty in relating Harry's world to the valley. Perhaps, however, I might have been moved and inspired by the books if I had been able to read them soon after spring 1968, because of the fact that Harry's parents are dead, and even Dumbledore, his surrogate father, dies in one of the later books. There was about to be a death in our family.

LAST DAYS

On the night of March 19 1968, my father got up in the night and for some reason fell down on the dark landing outside the bedroom. He may have tripped over something, or he may have had an attack of dizziness caused by the high blood pressure from which he suffered. He must have fallen very awkwardly and very hard, because, as we later discovered, he fractured one of his ribs. He stayed in bed all the next day, complaining of feeling more ill than usual, but forbidding my mother to fetch a doctor because of his dislike and distrust of the medical profession. On the day after, he was feverish and drifting in and out of consciousness, and my mother overruled his wishes and went to the local doctor, as well as contacting my father's sister and nephew. By the next morning, he was virtually comatose and the doctor decided to have him admitted to hospital. On a wild March morning with a strong wind coursing through the trees, I watched him being carried out to an ambulance on a stretcher. Perhaps because the men carrying him were unusually tall, or perhaps because of the unfamiliarity of the circumstances, my father suddenly seemed unusually small to my eyes. At the hospital we were eventually told that the broken rib had pierced his lung and that he had developed pneumonia.

At first, he seemed to be making a good recovery, regaining consciousness, sitting up in bed and able to talk to us, but quite suddenly his condition worsened. Seven days after being admitted to hospital, his condition seemed stable though serious, so that my mother and I, and later my brother also, went home for the night. My father died late in the evening of March 29 1968 and I have been told that in his last hours he regained consciousness and knew that he was going to die, and said so quite matter-of-factly. The hospital staff phoned Mr and Mrs Nozicka at North Lodge when they realised how little time my father had left, in order to call my mother to his bedside. I remember Mr Nozicka's van turning outside our house, its headlights pencilling through the darkness of the spring night, taking my mother off to the hospital. My father was dead before she arrived. Whatever motives my parents had had for coming to live at Upper Lodge and for staying there so long were irrelevant now. Whatever plans, hopes, or dreams they may have had for their life in the valley were now at an end. Almost immediately, my mother began making plans to move to the village.

There is an incident that happened about three years before my father's death that is characteristic of him, and it is also an illustration of the harsher side of our life in the valley, though it is only since I started to write this book that I have fully remembered it. I was about eight years old at the time, and I was playing in the trees a short distance from the house when I heard shouts and voices raised in anger and then the deafening, overawing crash of a gun being fired. I ran towards the noise and saw my father confronting three young men of about eighteen or twenty years old, all carrying shotguns. They were swearing and cursing at him in a rather hysterical, high-pitched way while he steadily shouted at them to leave. He may have caught them about to shoot some bird or animal right outside our house and understandably told them to move on because what they were doing was dangerous. I do not know where my brother was, but as it was the middle of the day, I am fairly certain he was at work. Suddenly, one of the young men raised his shotgun and fired straight at my father, or so it seemed to me, and I began to scream and cry in terror. My father moved forwards, straight towards the young man who had fired, stepping steadily and purposefully, his face red with anger as he went on shouting at them to leave. Prince the German shepherd had appeared and was circling the strangers, trying to attack. The other two youths were striking out and clubbing at the dog with their rifle butts, perhaps they would have shot him if they had not been so close to their friend, with the dog moving so quickly. The shot had gone over my father's head, either because the young man had deliberately aimed high, or because panic and fear had made him miss. Over the sound of my own sobbing I seemed to hear the gunshot echoing and echoing again in my head.

I was running more or less towards my father from behind, and I could hear the clash of Prince's teeth on the gun butts mixed with his furious barking as the young men rapidly backed away from my father and the dog. My mother had come out of the house now, also shouting, and the noise was indescribably terrifying. Suddenly, the same young man shot at my father again and everything and everyone seemed to freeze into stillness and silence for a moment. My mother grabbed the dog by the collar. This shot had gone wide and low and it ripped off the top of a tall weed not much more than a metre from my right leg. My father turned and saw me and let out a roar of pure rage and threw himself at the young men. They now began to run away from him, and I was aware of a strange sound. It was the sound of my father's boots thudding on the stony ground and it was strange because he never ran due to the state of his lungs. I watched my father charge at three young men who were about fifty years younger than himself, all of them armed with shotguns, his bare fists up, chasing three youths, one of them having already shot at him twice, on and on, trying desperately to catch them. There was another wild shot fired, I think by the same young man who had fired the first two, but I never knew how close it came to my father. At last, he stopped and doubled up, coughing and coughing convulsively and fighting for breath, so that the young men were able to run off into the woods and disappear.

My mother went to the police that day, and a police officer came to the house to take a statement from my father. The three young men were never found or arrested. Perhaps my father made light of the incident in his usual stubborn way when he spoke to the police officer, having considered that he had dealt with it in his own style, or perhaps the police did not give it any great importance, shrugging it off as the kind of thing that tended to happen in the valley, or perhaps the young men came from far outside the area and could not be found.

Several weeks after my father's death, I received the news that I had passed the selection process (there was no longer a single exam by that year) and would go to the grammar school in September. It was a strange summer, and an even stranger autumn followed it. For the first time in my childhood, my mother went out to work in the daytime, getting a job as a dinner lady in the village primary school that I had just left, so that with my brother also at work, the dogs were left alone in our house in the valley until we all returned in the late afternoon. We knew that we would be moving to a house in the village, but we did not know when, and so those months had the odd feeling of *no longer, but not yet*.

I had to walk into the village each school day morning, either by way of the drive or over the fields, a distance of between a mile and a mile and a half, before I could take the school bus to Gowerton where the red brick grammar school stood. Sometimes I missed the school bus, and unless there was someone around who knew my mother and could offer me a lift, there was no way of getting to school, or so I told myself. Somehow, I missed the school bus quite often, and on other days I was ill. For the first time in my life I was alone with the dogs in the house until evening. Strangely, these were very happy times. I ate the sandwiches that my mother had made me for school, or began to experiment with cooking for myself, and I wandered through the valley with the dogs as I had already been doing for years, or read for hours in the quiet house, listening to the radio when I tired of reading. Some days, I left the dogs behind and walked up into the village or south through the valley to the tiny village of Cadle Mill, and spent what money I had in shops in these places. Village shops sold more paperback books in those days than is usual now, and if I could afford it, my money went on a book, a packet of salted peanuts and a bottle of lemonade, a combination of pleasures that seemed close to sheer heaven to me at that age. *Night Without End* by Alistair MacLean, an exciting story of a plane crash in Greenland, and *A Town Like Alice* by Nevil Shute, a romance set in the Far East and Australia in wartime, popular novels and writers of the 1960s, largely forgotten today, provided me with a change from Tolkien and Jack London. Certainly, I still felt grief about my father's death, but this was no worse on the long days I spent alone with the dogs than at any other time. I was deeply content on those truant days, but on one of them I had one of the strangest encounters of my life, so that I have been puzzling over it for almost forty years.

It was an unusually warm and sunny morning around the beginning of March, almost a year after my father's death. At about eleven in the morning, I decided to take the dogs for a long walk, carrying a bag with some sandwiches, a drink and the inevitable book over my shoulder. The daffodils outside our house were budding, although the bracken on the slopes of the valley was very dry and brown as it had been all winter. Several paces from the back door, I stopped abruptly – a woman was standing on the drive outside our house. I made a grab for Prince because the German shepherd was invariably aggressive towards all strangers, but oddly, he stood watching her with hesitation, only growling slightly. The woman turned to look at me and I saw that she was a few years younger than my mother, perhaps in her mid-forties. I had been warned about the risks of strangers, but I was twelve now and I had a large, fierce dog with me, and after all, this was a woman on her own.

'Is your mother in?' the woman asked.

'No, she's at work. My brother is at work too.'

The woman looked at me searchingly, then suddenly started and put her hand to her mouth in a gesture of shock.

'Your father is dead, isn't he?'

'Yes.' I said, and looked away, as a matter of fact I had begun to be embarrassed by the expressions of sympathy and concern that came my way as a bereaved child. For some reason, I did not think of asking her how she knew about my father's death.

'The pain...' she said vaguely, seeming to be deep in thought.

'Do you know my mother?'

'Oh no, I've never met her. I never met your father either.' She stood there, seeming to consider something, and I saw that she was quite attractive, with quite long, wavy, black hair. At that moment, I realised that there was something strange about her eyes, not just their colour, which seemed to be green, but also their shape and how widely apart they were set. She wore a knee-length skirt of dark suede and short, brown boots, and also a green jacket, unbuttoned over a red blouse, and curiously, her clothes looked a little like some kind of uniform. She stepped forward and Prince snarled, but when she glanced at him, he became quiet.

'My name is Kerstin.'

'Kerstin?' I repeated the unfamiliar name to make sure I had got it right and avoid looking silly, and it was just at that moment that I realised there was the slight trace of a foreign accent in her words.

'Yes, Kerstin. What is your name?'

'Anthony.'

She stretched out her hand to me and Prince grunted uneasily, but didn't snarl, while my mongrel Tim was already wagging his tail and rubbing against her legs.

'I'm very pleased to meet you.' Kerstin said, ignoring the dogs. 'Now, I wonder if you would be willing to help me.'

'What do you want?' I said awkwardly. A strong wind began to blow and it flattened the daffodil stems almost against the ground, and the sunlight turned to grey as a cloud passed rapidly across the sun, bringing a hint of hail or rain into the air. Kerstin's eyes seemed to change colour quite dramatically as the light changed, and I noticed that there were a few silver and grey streaks in her hair.

'I'd like to walk all the way down the valley to Cadle Mill, but I'd like to walk along the river, as I used to do years ago, not along the drive past Middle Lodge. The trouble is that I don't know if I can find my way along the river and around the lake after all these years, so I'm afraid of getting lost.'

'The lake has been drained.'

'Really? Has it? I wonder why! Anyway, will you walk along with me and show me the way? You were going to take your dogs for a long walk, weren't you?'

'Yes, I was. Do you live around here then?'

'I live in England now. But I'm staying in Swansea for a few days. I used to live just outside Swansea before the war and during the war. I used to visit this valley, and so now I've come back. I lived abroad for years after the war and I often used to think of this place. Well, will you come with me, so that I don't get lost?' Kerstin's voice had an unusually soft, breathless quality, so that she seemed to caress the words that she pronounced in her slightly foreign way.

'Yes, alright. I'll come with you. But parts of it are very rough and overgrown.' I told her.

'I'm sure you'll get us through, Anthony.' Kerstin said. 'Of course, I'll need to stop and rest at times.' The cloud moved away now and we were flooded with warm sunshine again in a typical display of late winter weather.

As we walked down into the forest, I noticed how tall Kerstin was, considerably taller than me at that age.

'You are not in school today?'

'Well...No. I'm ill.' I said uneasily. Kerstin swept her fingers through her long, dark hair and looked at me with a wild, glittering, sideways smile.

'Well, I hope you recover soon.'

'Yeah. Thanks.'

'Is there still no bathroom in Upper Lodge?' Kerstin asked me, stopping and looking me squarely in the face.

'No. We have this big zinc bath and fill it with water that we heat up.' I felt my face redden with embarrassment because I had reached the age when it bothered me to admit how primitive our living conditions actually were.

'And that is what you were bathed in as a baby.' Kerstin said with a peculiar expression, seeming to search my face with her eyes. 'Sadly, I have never had children.'

We walked on past the place at the bottom of a sloping bank where my father and I had lit a fire and cooked bacon on it. Perhaps some sharp sense of grief passed through me and Kerstin sensed it. She stopped again and laid her hand on my arm and spoke to me gently.

'You won't always feel like this...Come on, I seem to remember there's a big yew tree further on, let's go and look!'

There was indeed a big yew tree at that time, and I had often cut small branches from it to make bows that I strung with thick twine, using arrows made from the bamboos standing in that dense expanse that Kerstin and I were now passing. When we reached the tree, she began chattering excitedly.

'Did you know that yew trees live for hundreds and hundreds of years? They are often planted in churchyards and sometimes people thought they were sacred. And of course, they made bows from the wood to shoot arrows.' She ended on a knowing smile, winking at me, and then she began to laugh at the dogs rolling and playing in the bracken where the sun was striking at the edge of the clearing. We moved off, and Kerstin was quiet for a long while, seeming to be deep in thought as we moved through places where the woodland was particularly thick in those days, the trees closing in around us as we got near to the bank of the river. As she had requested, I led her along the path that followed the river, so overgrown in places, even in winter, that it barely existed, or wound through boggy places and slippery patches of black mud, sometimes blocked by fallen trees that we had to climb over. At last, we came to the place where the lake had been that was now a broad expanse of yellowish brown reeds through which the river ran, and Kerstin began looking around her and shaking her head in disbelief. I also remembered the lake very well, but I had come here often since it had been drained and so had become used to the sight. When we were about halfway across the bed of the lake, Kerstin sat down on the river bank in the sunlight and took out a packet of cigarettes and lit one of them.

'I hope you don't smoke!'

'No.' I said truthfully. 'Never.'
'You shouldn't smoke, it's very, very bad for you.'
'Why do you do it then?'
'You pick up some silly habits when you grow up. I only smoke a cigarette once in a while, usually when I've had a shock, as I have just now. It's so different here without the lake!'

'I suppose so.' I said, as the dogs charged past me with their jaws clamped on the opposite ends of a dead branch and went crashing into the reeds.

'You see up there?' Kerstin pointed at the tawny hillside, covered in bracken, behind us and beyond the lake, rising to meet the keen blue of the sky. 'There was a manor house called Nydfwch on the top of that hill for hundreds of years, until it was pulled down.'

'There's nothing up there now.' I objected. 'Only Brynrhos Farm on the other side of the hill.'

'Yes, I know. The manor house was demolished. Why, who knows?'

'There are bumps in the ground up there, and some lumps of stone. I remember now.'

When Kerstin had finished her cigarette and put the packet back into the large handbag she carried, we walked the rest of the way across the reed beds and climbed the slope to a place where the river flowed between rearing walls of broken and overgrown masonry. Once again, she seemed amazed at the changes she saw, walking up and down, peering and shaking her head and sighing.

'This was the dam! Strange to see how they have breached it! Well, Anthony, I have some sandwiches and a drink in my handbag. Shall we sit down and rest and eat?'

'I've got some sandwiches and a drink too.'

'Then we shall share.'

We found a place beyond the dam where we could sit on a log in the warm sunshine, near the edge of the thick woodland that closed in again further down the river. I gave Kerstin two of my cheese and pickle sandwiches and she gave me two of hers, and I found that the sandwiches she had brought were made from something I had never tasted before. I asked her what it was.

'It's called houmous, and it's made from chickpeas and sesame seeds. They eat it in southern parts. Do you like it?'

I told her that I did, and that I had never tried it before. My mother had no interest in food that was not British, and I doubt that she could have bought houmous in South Wales in 1969, even in a large supermarket, even if she had wanted to. I drank my lemonade and Kerstin drank tonic water, which I did not like when she gave me some to try. The dogs sat near us, shifting their front legs impatiently and hoping for scraps. We ate and drank in a companionable silence, and then Kerstin reached out and wiped my face with her handkerchief.

'You had houmous on your chin.' she said softly.
'Thank you.'
'Well now, do you like to read? I think you must like reading. What do you like best?' Unlike most adults, the enthusiasm and earnestness that Kerstin radiated made her seem genuinely interested and eager to hear what I had to say.

'I like *The Lord of the Rings* by Tolkien. I'm reading it for the second time.'

'Yes, I read that once, but it frightens me. That Sauron, the Dark Lord! Just a Great Eye, watching and watching. Horrible!' Kerstin actually shuddered visibly and her own eyes seemed to change colour again.

'They destroy him in the end, though.'
'Yes. What else do you like to read?'
'I like to read Jack London's books.'
'Jack London? I've been to the place where he used to live in California. Did you know that he grew very rich from his writing and had his own big ranch?'

I nodded eagerly, and told her that I knew a lot about his life, finding it as interesting as his books. Kerstin smiled and went on.

'Yes, a big ranch, in a place called The Valley of the Moon, perhaps a little bit like the Dillwyn Llewelyn estate in this valley. I bought some of his books in America. When we meet next I must give them to you. I brought a box of unusual books with me to Swansea, thinking that I might sell them, but you might as well have the ones by Jack London. Would you like that?'

'Yes, please! Thank you very much!' I said breathlessly.
'And what did you like to read when you were younger?'
'I liked the stories about King Arthur when I was little.'
'What did you think of the story about the lady Morgan le Fay and the other three queens putting a spell on Sir Lancelot and keeping him prisoner in the castle and telling him he had to choose one of them as

his wife and stay there forever?'

'I suppose he had to get out because he was a knight.'

'He should have known when he was well off! He should have chosen one of them and stayed in the castle where he was safe!' Kerstin was becoming animated now. A jet fighter flew low over the valley from east to west, with a sudden roar that seemed to tear the sky open and made the dogs whine, and Kerstin frowned at it as she went on speaking. 'There is always trouble going on in some part of the world. Vietnam and Czechoslovakia, or some other place, always trouble and unhappiness. Do you read the newspapers, Anthony?'

'Not much, but I listen to the radio.'

'And did you hear about Czechoslovakia a few months ago?'

'Yes. Mr Nozicka who lives in North Lodge is from Czechoslovakia.'

'The world should be ruled by women!' Kerstin said passionately, plucking a long stem of dry grass from beside the log we were sitting on. 'Everywhere should be ruled by women, and then people would be safe and happy. Women know what is best.'

I didn't have the confidence at that age to discuss this with her, and her feelings seemed to have become so aroused that I was afraid of upsetting her if I said anything. She became thoughtful again now, but she soon brushed the crumbs from her skirt and stood up and spoke brightly and cheerfully again.

'Well, perhaps you and your dogs will guide me the rest of the way to Cadle Mill.'

The woodland was dense in this part of the valley, and the ground was even rougher than before, becoming very slippery in places because of the winter rains. I got the impression that Kerstin had not walked this far for a long time, and I saw her wince when she stepped over the trunk of a fallen tree and I thought she had hurt herself. Next moment, she stopped and hitched up her skirt on one side and fastened her stocking, and I saw a glimpse of white petticoat and white suspender. I stared and then looked away in boyish embarrassment.

She stopped a few minutes later and leaned against a tree, taking out her cigarettes and lighting one.

'Haile Selassie, who was once the emperor of Ethiopia used to visit the Big House during the war. He lived in this country. I met him once, very briefly.' Kerstin seemed both sad and tired now.

'The Big House was blown up when I was little.' I spoke delicately, not wanting to upset her feelings.

'So I saw when I walked past the place before I got to your house. Everything is so different, so very different.'

'Why did the emperor leave Ethiopia?'

'I think it was because the Italians invaded his country. I told you, always trouble and fighting everywhere. The world should be ruled by women. Well, let's go on, we must be close now.'

About ten minutes later, we reached Cadle Mill, and I called the dogs to me and put them both on their leads, looking curiously at Lower Lodge just beyond the trees and wondering if there was anyone around.

'I know exactly where I am now.' Kerstin said. 'I can get the bus from here back into Swansea. Thank you so very much for guiding me. But I want to give you those books. Do you think you might still be too ill to go to school again tomorrow?'

'I might be worse.' I said with a grin. 'Or I might miss the school bus.' I noticed Kerstin's quick and wicked smile, her face suddenly wild.

'Then I'll meet you here at twelve midday, exactly here at twelve. Will that be alright? Perhaps we can walk and talk some more.'

'Yes, I'll be here.' I started to turn away.

'It's the right thing where I come from to kiss when you leave a friend.' Kerstin said kindly and held her arms open to me. I dropped the leads and came to her and kissed her very awkwardly, smelling her perfume and the scent of tobacco that suggested that she smoked more than she admitted. She walked off through the trees towards the houses and the road, stopping once to wave to me.

On the following day, I arrived at the same spot more than half an hour early and stayed for over three hours, but Kerstin did not appear. I went there on the next day and the next at the same time and waited for a similar period without seeing her. It was no hardship to sit by the river and eat sandwiches and read, especially as the weather remained fine, but I was disappointed about not getting the books by Jack London. I never saw Kerstin again and I never knew how much of what she told me about herself was true, and I have never been sure what her real motives were. On the other hand, I know that the things she told me about the Penllergare Valley Woods were true because I later checked them with reliable sources. The day with Kerstin was a turning point of a strange kind, and after it I always felt somewhat older, further from my childhood.

Although I was only twelve, there was something about those last days in the valley woods, some kind of unrest or vulnerability in me that drew people to talk to me. I had another encounter and heard another long story one sunny Saturday morning at the end of the month of March, almost exactly a year after my father's death, though this one was not as strange as the meeting with Kerstin.

Perhaps because the first anniversary of my father's death was on my mind, I walked up into the village to call on my friend Tony Gilbank. Sadly, he had gone to the secondary modern school in Pontardulais, and I did not see much of him anymore. As it turned out, I was not to see him on that morning because I found the whole family out when I knocked on his door. So I wandered back towards the valley, but decided to go to the Midway Cafe on the road to Morriston, a place where motorists and lorry drivers stopped for tea, coffee or fried food. There was no M4 motorway cutting through the area in those days, only a fast stretch of road that crossed the river on the stone Melin Llan Bridge, later demolished. I bought myself a coke, feeling very free and very grown up, and sat down at one of the tables to drink it. There were very few people in the cafe, but I did notice a young woman of about twenty-three with her long blonde hair tied back, wearing jeans and with a large rucksack by her feet. She looked slightly familiar and she seemed to be watching me as she drank her coffee.

'Don't you live in one of the lodges in the valley woods?' the young woman asked me after a few minutes.

'Yes. That's right. How did you know?' I was less shy and awkward after the day I had spent with Kerstin. The coke was cold and tingling in my throat, and the lorries were roaring by in the spring sunshine outside while here in the cafe I was talking to another adult.

'My dad used to take my sister and me for walks near your house. We stopped and talked to your parents sometimes. Sorry, I've forgotten your name.'

'Anthony. Isn't your name Karen?'

'That's right. How are your parents?' Karen leaned back, putting her coffee down and tightening the simple band that gathered her blonde hair into a ponytail.

'My father died a year ago.'

'I'm very, very sorry.' Karen paused, and looked embarrassed for a moment before going on. 'We found a stray black cat in the woods once and took him home. At least, he seemed to be a stray. My mum has still got him. I hope he wasn't yours.'

'No, we've never had a cat. I'm glad you rescued him, the foxes would have got him otherwise.' I realised that I sounded more confident, even to myself, than I had before I had met Kerstin.

'I'm on my way home.' Karen said and sighed and stretched out her legs, and then she touched the rucksack anxiously, as if she was making sure it was still there. 'Last stage! I've been travelling across Europe, all the way to Austria. I've been staying with an Australian girl who helped me out.'

Karen was immediately transformed into a romantic heroine in my eyes. I had never travelled abroad at that time, but I longed to do so. I had also heard stories of daring young people who hitchhiked across one country after another, with rucksacks on their backs, and this was very much part of the mood of the sixties, the extraordinary decade that was coming to an end now. Suddenly, I was confronted with a young woman who had come for walks in our little valley and had gone on to have these adventures.

'Where do you go to school now?' Karen asked suddenly.

'Gowerton.' I told her.

'I have friends who went to the Girls' Grammar School there. Any idea what you want to do when you leave school?' Karen's fresh, unassuming manner and the way she treated me like an equal raised this question above the level of that most predictable of adult questions, *what do you want to be when you grow up?*

'I think perhaps I'd like to be a journalist or a writer of some kind.' I told her seriously. She sipped her coffee and seemed to be considering.

'Alright. If you're interested, I'll tell you about something that happened to me last month in France. When you go home, you can write it down and maybe you can use it.' Karen offered.

She bought herself another coffee and a coke for me and she told me her story. It showed just how intensely someone could carry the memory of the Penllergare Valley Woods as a special place while travelling far away. I did indeed write it down. Long before I was twelve, I began the lifelong habit of filling diaries and notebooks with descriptions of incidents and conversations I had with many kinds of people, so that I could preserve what my already unusually exact memory retained. In my next chapter, *The Paris Train and the Black Cat*, I tell Karen's story based on her own words.

* * *

About three weeks after the day I met Karen in the Midway Cafe, I stood at the bottom of Swede's Field with the spring storms and sunlight chasing each other in circles down the valley, feeling an enormous sadness and apprehension. I had been sent out to exercise the dogs while frantic activity went on back at the house, and I knew that everything had changed and our life here in the valley was over, so that it was one of those moments when the present already seems like the past. The removal van was coming soon and we were finally leaving Upper Lodge. I was already developing the bookish and introspective person's habit of thinking in quotations, but at that age I didn't have a great store of good ones to draw upon.

During the Easter holiday we had gone to see a film in one of the Swansea cinemas. I remember the red double-decker bus, the conductor with his leather satchel of coins, the ornate stairway of the cinema, the carpets, potted plants, framed photographs of Hollywood stars, and the taste of ice cream sold by a lady with a torch during the intermission. The film was *Gone With The Wind*, something I find a little embarrassing to watch today, having made friends of all races and colours during my life. As I stood in the field on that stormy April day, on the last day I would ever live in the valley woods, some words from the film came back to me. *'Look for it only in books, for it is no more than a dream remembered. A civilisation gone with the wind...'*

THE PARIS TRAIN AND THE BLACK CAT

Now, everyone would say: I told you so! I told you it was too dangerous! Karen kept thinking this over and over again and it was probably the worst thing in this awful situation. She was in a foreign city on a damp February evening with no money and nowhere to sleep and no way to get home, at least not without turning to someone for help and not without an enormous amount of trouble. In her imagination, the reproachful voices of her friends and family, all telling her that travelling right across Europe and back by bus and train was far too dangerous for a young woman of twenty-three, rose and fell like the roar of an angry, distant crowd. She had always wanted to travel, longed to see foreign places, and the yearning had started on those walks with her father and her sister in those valley woods that were full of strange trees and plants and mysterious ruins.

For the tenth time, she cursed herself for being so careless. Just the thing she had promised herself that *she* would never do! It was just that she had been so tired when she got on the train in Paris. It was also a city that she felt relieved to get out of because it seemed to be still seething sullenly after the riots in the previous May. So, instead of putting her wallet, containing all her cash and traveller's cheques, together with her train ticket and her ferry ticket, safely in the belt bag around her waist, she had just put it in her rucksack, which was on her lap. Just as soon as the ticket inspector had come around, Karen's eyes had been closing with sheer weariness and she had stuffed the wallet into her rucksack without properly closing the top, then she had fallen fast asleep.

The whole trip had gone so well until then. Karen, after three years of hard work in college, always wanting to be daring and different, had travelled all the way to Austria, stopping wherever she wished. Oddly, the valley woods had come back to her in her dreams at night far more often than her own home. It was the adventure of a lifetime, saved for so hard. And now, after a magical autumn and winter, this had to happen! Just when she was only two days from home. She had enjoyed looking over the famous cathedral here in Rouen in northern France, which towered over the centre of the city like some giant in a black suit of armour. As she came out of the cathedral, it was already getting dark and she felt into her belt bag for her wallet...and remembered.

Karen had a sensation that felt like her stomach falling through her boots and the earth falling away under her feet. She searched her rucksack from top to bottom right there on the cathedral steps. There was no doubt about it, either some horrible light-fingered individual had taken her wallet out of the top of her rucksack, or – less likely – it had fallen out onto the carriage floor.

She ran across town back to the railway station. Of course, the enquiries office was closed, but she did get one of the staff selling tickets to check if a wallet had been found on the train from Paris (now hundreds of miles away) and handed in. *No, mademoiselle, very sorry mademoiselle.* The young man who sold tickets seemed a nice guy and for a moment Karen considered blurting out the whole sorry story to him, but a mixture of pride and confusion stopped her. She knew that if she told him, she would begin to cry. Instead, she walked back across town, with her head bowed sadly, her blonde hair tied back.

The proprietor of the little bar sighed into his grey moustache. Karen was his only customer and he was restless to close for the day. The only money she had left was some loose change in the pockets of her jeans and she had decided to spend it on a coffee and a glass of wine. Of course, there were lots of cheap places to stay in a city like Rouen in February, so she hadn't booked anywhere in advance. She had counted on having money! She had no idea where the British embassy or consulate was in Rouen. Would it even be open at this hour? They got you home, didn't they? But didn't they charge you for it afterwards? Of course, her father or mother or *someone* would get her some money eventually, but her parents were not well off and would find it a blow. And the embarrassment of having to ask! *I told you so, I told you so.* The words jangled like keys in her head. Well, there were three good things. One, she still had her passport in her belt bag and could prove who she was. Two, her whole rucksack hadn't been stolen, so she still had some clean underwear. And three...it was hard to think of a third thing. Oh yes, she could still buy a bar of chocolate. Karen quickly counted her remaining coins in the palm of her hand. No, she couldn't afford a bar of chocolate. Cancel Good Thing Number Three, then. Banks and offices would be open tomorrow, but what about tonight? For one thing where would she sleep? She could see through the steamy window of the little bar that it was raining outside. She had to decide what to do. For some reason, she found her mind drifting back to the Midway Cafe where her father sometimes took her after walks by the Llan river and to the colour of the rhododendrons in early summer.

'Still open then, Gustave?' The voice was loud, female and had an Australian accent. Karen looked up and saw that a young woman of about her own age in a denim miniskirt, very nice boots and tights and a leather jacket over a sparkly top, had just walked into the bar. The proprietor answered the Australian girl by rolling his eyes towards the ceiling and spreading his hands. Next, the young woman came over to Karen's table. She had short, bouncy, dark hair, quite unlike Karen's long blonde hair and she was pretty and tanned.
'Hi, are you British?'
'Yeah.' Karen said. 'How did you know?'
'Ah, jest intuition, I guess. I'm Angela. I've been working in another bar across town for the last six months. Last day today, I'll soon be gone like President de Gaulle. I'm going home tomorrow.'
Angela put her hand out and Karen shook it and introduced herself, all the while thinking: *I'm glad getting home is so simple for some people.*
'Can I buy you another glass of wine?' Angela asked. 'I'm kinda celebrating tonight.'
'No thanks. I was just leaving.' Karen said, feeling almost resentful that the Australian girl was distracting her from the comforting images of the valley woods.
'Ah well. Another time. Well, I must jest go to the little girls' room.'

As Angela disappeared, Karen began to gather up her things. Feeling so sorry for herself, but also so embarrassed, as well as too proud to ask for help, the last thing Karen wanted was the company of this pretty, cool, super-confident Australian girl. She was just about to stand up when a great deal of noise by the door stopped her. About ten young men walked in, all of them a bit drunk, a mixture of Americans, British and French, talking excitedly. When they saw a young woman in her early twenties with blonde hair, sitting alone at a table, they began to shout and call out. Karen had a lot of confidence in herself after travelling all the way to Austria and back, but she couldn't pretend to herself that she wasn't rather scared. She steadily ignored the young men and tried to judge the best moment to walk past them and out of the bar without stirring up further trouble. But the shouting and calling went on.

Suddenly, Angela was standing beside Karen's table. In very fluent French and in a voice that seemed cold and sharp enough to slice diamonds, Angela scolded the young men like a teacher in front of a class of eight year-olds. They had all fallen silent now and looked embarrassed. Gustave, the proprietor of the bar, who seemed to be a friend of Angela's, folded his arms as a sign that he would not serve the young men. Gradually, looking at each other uneasily, they all left without another word.

'Wow.' Karen said. 'That was something to see.'

'Ah, jest comes from the experience of working in a bar. Lot of big kids!'

'What did you say to them?'

'I told the French guys that you are a guest in their country and so they ought to have more respect. And I told the British and American guys that they are guests in France and they need to behave themselves.'

'Seemed to work.'

'Usually does. Look, I think our friend Gustave here wants to close for the night. There's another cafe a little way off that's still open. Why don't I walk along with you?'

Karen couldn't help thinking that the gang of young men might well be still outside in the street and getting more bad-tempered, and quickly accepted this offer. Also, she was starting to like Angela more and more by the minute.

Two streets further on, they turned a corner and passed a woman in a very short red raincoat and skirt shouting at two French policemen.

'There's an old legend in this town about a black cat.' Angela was saying. 'People who meet the cat always travel home safely and without trouble.'

'Sounds like a lot of rubbish to me.' Karen told her. She was thinking of the cat that she and her sister had found under that huge copper beech in the valley, the one they had taken home and adopted. As a matter of fact, she was still trying to decide where she could sleep tonight and how to sort the entire mess out and she found it difficult to think as Angela kept chattering. She wondered whether to tell Angela about the trouble she was in – at least Angela didn't seem the kind of girl to just walk away or to be smug and superior either.

'Here's the cafe.' Angela said. 'Buy you a beer?'

Karen agreed and they went inside. There was a middle-aged woman behind the bar and three elderly men playing cards and drinking red wine. *No international gangs of young trouble-makers, at least I'm getting some good luck today,* Karen thought. When she took a mouthful of the very cold beer, she felt it going to her head after the glass of wine she had drunk earlier.

'You seem so serious and solemn, Karen. Are all British girls like you?'

Karen didn't answer her. The wine and the mouthful of beer were making everything seem a bit cloudy and for a moment her eyelids fluttered down and she felt sleep getting close, just as she had on the Paris train that day when she had made the stupid mistake that had started all this. Then suddenly, she felt something sliding softly against her leg under the table. Karen actually screamed and jumped in her chair and then stood up quickly. The three elderly men looked up from their card game and raised their eyebrows and sighed. Then, from under the table, there emerged a large black tomcat with a white stripe along the middle of his head. Karen could feel her hands shaking and sat down again.

'Only a cat.' Angela said cheerfully. 'I told you about the legend, didn't I? Now you're sure to travel safely. Your nerves seem bad, though.'

'I've had a difficult day.' Karen told her.

'You really seem to have the weight of the world on your shoulders, don't you, Karen? Nothing is as bad as it seems.'

'Some things are.' Karen answered sadly, looking at the floor. Angela grinned before speaking.

'What? You mean, like losing your wallet on a train and probably all your money and your ticket home?'

Karen felt her face go white and a cold chill run down her back and a little flame of fear prickle in her stomach. After the appearance of the cat, this situation was becoming seriously, sickeningly alarming.

'How did you know that?' Karen asked in a shaking whisper.

'Not difficult.' Angela seemed to be enjoying herself. 'I saw you at the railway station. I'd been seeing some friends off and I heard you asking that young guy at the ticket office about your wallet. You seemed frantic. Then you just went striding off. Well, it's not difficult to follow a blonde British girl looking utterly miserable across this city.'

'But you said nothing!' Karen snapped.

'Ah, come on, Karen! You hardly gave me a chance, did you? You weren't exactly friendly when I offered to buy you a drink at the other bar. Then those young guys turned up. Anyway, let me tell you something else. I'm moving to England tomorrow, *with* my parents. They're arriving from Spain in their own car and we're driving all the way. Come with us. Please accept, it's not like it's going to cost us anything.'

Karen stood up, her voice shrill.

'Angela, you are a – '

'What?'

'Probably a person who is going to be a very good friend of mine.' Karen told her, leaning on the table.

'Great. Well, if you don't mind a spare sleeping bag on the sofa, you can sleep at the place I've been renting. It's my last night there, be nice to have company. And if you're hungry, I make a mean pizza.'

'One condition.' Karen said, as they finished their beer and began to leave the bar.

'What's that?'

'No more black cat legends... On the other hand, if we're going to be friends and you are coming to Britain, maybe you'd like to visit a valley in South Wales that I know. It's like Rouen, a good place for finding cats.'

* * *

About two years after we left Upper Lodge, I met Karen and Angela walking in the valley woods one winter day, and found Angela to be exactly as Karen described her, and also both impressed and bemused by the valley. Sadly, I later lost all touch with Karen, but the name Karen is one I have always liked and used in my writing. In 1986, I was in Rouen for some time. I didn't find anyone who remembered Angela or Karen, but I was told that there used to be a bar kept by a man called Gustave.

AFTERLIFE

Our truck hurtled forward along the rutted track of loose stones, and already the Land Rover ahead of us was hidden in the cloud of dust being kicked up by its own wheels. I looked sideways at the other two men in the truck and could see that they were slightly tense and nervous by the drawn intensity of their faces, and also from the way in which one of them was gripping the steering wheel as he drove. He was a good driver, but he feared crashing into the back of the Land Rover ahead, and we had all been a bit taken aback by our glimpse of the forest fire from further up the valley a few minutes ago. We were now racing towards the demonic, red and black centre of energy that we had glimpsed a little way back, led by the man in the vehicle ahead of us, who probably was too reckless to be nervous about anything.

It was early April 1974, and this was my first big forest fire, having broken out on the east side of the valley in coniferous forest not far from the drained lake, on Forestry Commission land. I stepped down from the still moving truck as the driver wrenched up the hand brake, the smoke cutting at my throat, my eyes rebelling and spilling, feeling the heat push into my face and chest. The wind was coming in gusts about three seconds apart, like the unhurried, regular strokes of an axe, and with each gust another tree, four or five metres tall, would flare up from top to bottom with a hiss. For a second, I felt the heat and just stared.

'Get at it there, on the edge of that clearing! Stop it spreading on that side!' There were shouts all around me, then I was running forward with two other men, attacking the blazing vegetation with beaters, wooden handles about as tall as ourselves onto which were fixed square flaps of reinforced rubber. Some time later – minutes or half an hour – I was leaning on my beater and slowly grasping the fact that we had quelled the forest fire. It was out – the monster had been subdued. I felt oddly detached and free of emotion.

I had been unhappy at school and had not done well there (indeed, I did not take my degree at university until 1991, as a mature student of thirty-four) and so just after my seventeenth birthday I got a job with the Forestry Commission, often working in the same valley in which I had grown up and feeling that my life continued to be bound up with the place.

After we left Upper Lodge in April 1969, there was not much that changed for some years, except that Upper Lodge and Middle Lodge were demolished quite soon and the rubble was removed load by load. I came back to the valley woods frequently, and building and development in the area of the valley did not increase much or change the look of things for a few years. One Sunday morning in spring, about two years after we moved, I was standing near the remains of my childhood home, now no more than an overgrown section of wall, watching the sun breaking through the mist that still lay in white, drifting patches in the hollows of the valley, so that the grass was glistening steamily. Someone came around the bend in the drive near the place where our home had once stood.

'Hello, Tony! You come back to see your house?' It was Mr Nozicka from North Lodge, out with his dog, and as always he pronounced my name 'tawny'.

'Yeah. Not much left of it, is there?' We stood staring at the ruin in silence, a fourteen year-old boy and a tall, lean man in a black beret with a proud, sad, deeply lined face.

'Knocked it down quick enough, for sure!' Mr Nozicka said.

'Why did they knock it down and take the stones away?'

'Well, they are good stones, Tony, always useful...' Mr Nozicka shrugged, suggesting that the answer was self-evident and part of the way of the world. 'It makes you sad I think.'

'I suppose so, but I often come back.'

'You grew up here, and that will always draw you back.'

As he said this, there was a terrible, indescribable sadness in his own voice, and I sensed all the weight of a divided and disrupted Europe in this man who could not go back to his native Czechoslovakia. I am delighted to say that Mr Nozicka lived to see the enormous changes in Eastern Europe after 1989, so that he did return to what became the Czech Republic on several visits, taking Mrs Nozicka with him. At the age of forty, I was able to spend some time in Prague, that most western of Eastern European cities and get to know something of its atmosphere and the character of its people.

In 1972, the huge DVLA centre was built just outside Morriston and from the valley woods at night the vast illuminated crane on the site was seen rearing up on the horizon. In the middle of the 1970s, a dual carriageway replaced the road that led out of the village, a road that had once wound between rather overgrown hedgerows past Cadle Mill and on towards Swansea. Just beyond Cadle Mill there grew up a huge complex of supermarkets and department stores from the late seventies onwards, while to the north of the valley the M4 motorway was extended and local government offices were built on site of the Dillwyn Llewelyn big house. The Observatory was, however, preserved and even restored. Something else did disappear and cannot be restored – the quiet of the valley as it was in my childhood. Even on the most peaceful days, there is some distant roar from the traffic of a society that no longer fully sleeps at any time.

In Orwell's novel *Coming up for Air*, the central character George Bowling, now a man in his forties, returns in the 1930s to the country village he has grown up in, only to find it simply swallowed up by a large manufacturing town and its housing estates and industrial complexes. This has never quite happened to the Penllergare Valley Woods, besieged and beleaguered though it has been by the speed of the changes nearby. Not quite! There has been much that has been preserved and there is much that can be preserved. Even so, awareness of what is precious grows very slowly, and the price of preserving the past, like the proverbial price of liberty, is eternal vigilance.

It is a hot summer night and I am lying in a sleeping bag under a huge tree in the valley. Four days ago, I locked up the flat I rent in the centre of Swansea and came here to the valley woods, carrying food and drink in a rucksack on my back and happily sleeping rough in a different clearing in the forest each night, keeping the mosquitoes away by a mixture of insect repellent and the smoke of small campfires. Despite the good weather, I meet very few people, and I spend my days tracing and retracing the paths and clearings of the valley and, in effect, my own memories and my own childhood...Kerstin, Karen, my parents and brother, our dogs, Malcolm Thomas the farmer, Mr and Mrs Nozicka, my friend Tony Gilbank and the other boys who sometimes came to call on me in the summertime as I grew older, the firemen and the man on the motor scooter on the day our chimney caught fire, my first teacher Miss Thomas and Miss Christine Hedges,

Linda Williams and her sisters in Middle Lodge and the iron severity of the winter of 1963, the radio programmes and the books and stories. Earlier this evening I found the patch of wild watercress and picked some to eat with my remaining food. It is dusk and I gradually fall asleep, only to awake some time later with my heart pounding in a state of terrible panic. For some reason I am desperate to get out of the valley – in a state of terror. I pack up my sleeping bag and possessions and walk and walk, out of the valley and back to Swansea...It was summer 1978, a time when Madonna had never been heard of, Muhammad Ali was still to win the world title for the third time, the Berlin Wall still had not fallen and Mr Nozicka could not return to the country of his birth. I have never understood the reason for that strange and unexpected state of panic. There were certainly huge changes still to come in the valley woods, in my own life and in the world in general.

I kept returning to the valley just as I had done in my years at grammar school when the place provided a comfort for my unhappiness at school. In the late winter of 1984, at a particularly painful time in my personal life, I spent each day for a fortnight in the woods, not sleeping outdoors, but walking there from morning until night, and rereading the books that had aroused my imagination in childhood. In the autumn of 1988, after my first visit to Finland, I buried a piece of pink Finnish granite under an oak tree in the valley as a tribute to the days when I first became fascinated by the most forested country in Europe because of the music I listened to on the radio in our home and because of my mother's memories of the Second World War that still made its presence felt in my young life. A few months later, my daughter Emma was born and Europe changed profoundly, so that it seemed that the unfinished business of a war that had affected my parents so much was finally concluded.

For most of the years from summer 1991 to autumn 1993, I lived in rural Andalucia in southern Spain, an area of deep ravines and river valleys, and coniferous forests mixed with mountain desert. My childhood made me feel almost completely at home in this area, not least because of the fact that many of the houses suffered from a poor water supply and the lack of running water for several hours each day during the summer. Also, the living conditions in many of the rural homes were primitive in other ways, and forest fires in summer, *el infierno*, often very widespread, were very serious matters indeed, regarded with dread. I could understand the attitudes and problems of the Andalucians and of the British and German exiles who chose to live among them, farming on a subsistence level on tiny *fincas*, peasant farms. I also realised how urban and industrialised South Wales and southern England are compared to Spain. The chances of a country village being simply swallowed up in a large urban area, like the village of Orwell's George Bowling and many real places, are much, much smaller in Spain, where villages tend to be swallowed by the enormity of *el campo*, the countryside. Like the Scandinavian countries, in which I have also travelled extensively in the last twenty-five years, open spaces are far more plentiful in Spain, so that existing spaces are not pressed on from every side.

On one of our short return visits to South Wales in the early 1990s, I heard that new building and development were being planned in the area of the Penllergare Valley Woods and I drew up a letter urging caution and care for the valley in the face of these plans. I spent a day in the area, going from house to house, knocking on doors and asking people to sign a petition attached to the letter to express their support, as this seemed to be at least something practical that I could do for the valley of my childhood. I was amazed to find that almost every person I approached was willing to sign the petition, and I later heard that the letter was read out at a local government meeting held to consider planning permission. I was soon back in Spain, but I hoped that my brief efforts had done some good.

It seems to me that having children gives us a sense of continuity, a sense of life going on, more than anything else in our lives. My daughter Emma began travelling and camping in the wild places of Europe when she was three weeks old, and she has shared my passion for remote places. Inevitably, she began to go to the valley woods from a young age, and wherever she was as a child she tended to prefer adventures with swords to games with dolls, though unlike myself she was always successful at school, never failed to attend, and went straight from school to university. On wild afternoons when the trees have been stripped of their leaves by the wind, or on oppressively hot summer days, throbbing with the noise of insects, with exotic trees and plants in bloom, we have made our way along the Llan, acting out strenuous games of make-believe similar to the ones I played in childhood, often inspired by the same books and stories.

In the last decade, I have been preoccupied with my own interests, and frequently travelling outside Britain, and it was not until late 2004, at an educational event in which my daughter, then aged fifteen, was taking part, that I met Mr Andrew Lloyd, who had attended the same primary school and grammar school as myself. I first heard of the Penllergare Trust from him, and was told about their plans to bring the valley woods to the attention of a wider public, so that it became obvious that awareness of the need to preserve that strange and beautiful place had grown enormously. Everything is always in a state of change, and from this comes permanent sadness and also permanent hope. Some of the people I remember most vividly and have described in this book have died in recent years, such as both Mr and Mrs Nozicka and my boyhood friend Tony Gilbank, a person I lost touch with completely in adult life. I have not seen some of the other people recalled in these pages for almost forty years and I have no idea where they are.

A great deal of what is built by human beings does not last, such as the towns and villas of Roman Britain and some of the homes on the estate of the Dillwyn Llewelyn family, while the things made by geology and nature, such as river valleys, do remain. In human terms, the landscape remains forever. It seems that the population of Britain and the rest of Europe is no longer expanding, and that in fact it is not even reaching replacement levels in many places, so that the need for new homes and living space will ultimately grow less. In the far distant future, the valley in which I grew up may grow larger and larger as a green place of trees and grass and quiet. Also, forty or fifty years from now, there may be people recalling how great a part the place played in their childhood days.

I continue to visit the valley and for many years I have continued to dream of it, but two dreams come more often than any others. In the first dream, the rooks are flying low over the house and the air is full of their clattering cries, and if I step out of the house the happiest moments of my childhood will be waiting for me. In the second dream, the valley is unrecognisable, there are buildings from horizon to horizon, not a single tree or a blade of grass anywhere, although I know that it is the same place. Like Orwell's George Bowling, I have returned to find the place of my childhood transformed and erased. If the first dream will never come true and will remain only a dream, at least the second has so far been only a nightmare.

ENDING AND BEGINNING

My wife and daughter went to an afternoon party on a Saturday in June, a party at which lingerie, toiletries and other girlie products were going to be exhibited and sold, and so it was not the kind of social occasion that I would fit into very well. In any case, I had better things to do. They left me at the huge twenty-four hour supermarket in the shopping complex near Cadle Mill, and I went in and bought some sandwiches and a bottle of cheap German wine, reflecting that this supermarket had not been built in my childhood, nor did such stores even exist. It was a beautiful day, and there was brilliant sunshine everywhere, but it was not particularly hot because a fresh wind was blowing. Cadle Mill was largely unchanged, though the little shop in which I used to buy lemonade and cheap books as a boy had closed down many years ago.

When I passed Lower Lodge, walking over the spot where I had seen Kerstin turn and wave, I saw that the house seemed to be in better repair than I ever remembered it. I followed the river and then the gravelled track that led northwards towards the lake, a path that did not exist when I lived in the valley. At last, there was the lake, not the huge bed of reeds that shocked Kerstin so much, but a real lake once again, a sheet of water reflecting the sunlight and the clear June sky and furrowed every few moments by the wind, like the expression on a face of someone frowning from time to time in concentration. I wandered along the edge of the lake for some time and then sat down by the water and read for a long time. The wind was doing a good job of keeping the insects away and there seemed to be no-one at all out in the valley that day, so that nothing disturbed my reading. Finally, I looked up at the hillside rising in the west beyond the lake on which the manor house of Nydfwch had once stood, its origins going back to the thirteenth century, and as the book I had been reading was about the Middle Ages, I had an intense feeling of once again sitting in the invisible presence of the past.

I went on up the river, keeping away from the place where my home had once stood because so much had changed within a few steps of it. The woodland and undergrowth were less dense in the valley than they had been in my childhood, so that the arch of the old stone bridge over which the drive went was visible from the river bank, and I remembered that tiny stalactites had formed in the masonry of the arch. The rhododendrons seemed more impressive than ever, gashing the dark greens of the valley with bursts of pink, scarlet and cream blooms. I stopped by the waterfall and ate my sandwiches and drank the wine, and finally someone did appear, a young man with two little girls, who was having a hard time keeping his children from wading into the river.

After leaving the waterfall, I walked up into the village to meet my wife and daughter as arranged, staring at the buildings of the primary school as I waited for them, the blue of the day turning grey as evening approached. The school buildings and the playground looked much the same as ever, but they seemed to have shrunk unbelievably.

'You ought to come and see the rhododendrons before they fade.' I told my wife and daughter when the talk of what they had bought at the party had subsided.

The following Saturday, we all went to the valley, taking the same route along the river as I had taken the week before. Emma, my daughter, seemed to revert to her childhood and climbed a large tree, perhaps to take her mind off all the things that had to be done in preparation for going to university in a few months. My wife Brenda took a photograph of me sitting in the forest with her mobile phone and afterwards kept it as a screen saver. This would have been science fiction, sheer science fiction in my childhood! At the waterfall, I had a serious conversation with Emma about how she might use the place for scenes for a film. Places that had once been settings for games were now looked at through the eyes of the young woman who had already started to make short films and wanted to direct them in the future. The waterfall has a main cataract and two smaller ones on each side of it, and I described how, despite my fear of heights, I used to jump across the smaller cataract on the western side and onto a flat rock, continuing to do this well into adult life.

'That was stupid.' Brenda said. 'If you'd fallen, I would never have met you.'

At the north end of the valley, we all sat on a stone wall above the huge concrete arch into which the river flowed, quite near the Midway Cafe where Karen had told me about her experiences in France. We took out wine, bread, Norwegian cheese and red peppers and began to eat a picnic, with the dog circling shiftily and hoping for scraps. Fish jumped at insects and slapped back into the river in widening circles of ripples.

'Did I tell you about cooking bacon with my father on the day he tried to catch fish?'

'Yes.' Brenda and Emma said together as they ate.

'The winter of 1963?'

'Yes, you did.' The siren of a fire engine could be heard out on the road.

'The day our house caught fire?'

They looked up at me and waited for me to begin.